CHILL

The Wine Lover's Introduction to Cannabis

Jackie McAskill

INGENIUM BOOKS

FIRST EDITION

ISBNs:
eBook: 978-1-990688-24-9
Hardcover: 978-1-990688-42-3
Paperback: 978-1-990688-23-2
Audiobook: 978-1-990688-25-6

ABOUT THE PUBLISHER

Ingenium Books Publishing Inc.
Toronto, Ontario, Canada M6P 1Z2.
All rights reserved.
ingeniumbooks.com

Edited by Amie McCracken
Cover design by Fresh Designs
Cover illustration by Stranger & Stranger
Interior illustrations by Thomas Beck

Disclaimer: The information provided in this book is for educational purposes only and should not replace professional advice—either legal or medical.

This book aims to provide comprehensive information and insights into the world of cannabis. However, laws and regulations concerning cannabis vary across countries, provinces, states, and regions. This book neither endorses nor promotes illegal activities related to cannabis or wine use. Readers are encouraged to understand and abide by the laws in their jurisdiction regarding cannabis.

CONTENTS

Introduction

I LOVE EVERYTHING ABOUT WINE. IT IS MEMORY MADE PHYSICAL (AND drinkable). It is a place and time in a glass. My favourite Pinot Noir brings me back to the wedding day I shared with my wife. A California Cabernet Sauvignon reminds me of a difficult conversation with my friend that made our relationship stronger in the end. Plus . . . delicious!

I spent more than fifteen years in the alcoholic beverage industry (insiders say, "alcohol beverage industry"), most of them as a buyer for the purchasing arm of one of the world's largest beverage alcohol retailers, a chain of stores owned by the Ontario government. While I worked with everything from coolers to spirits to beer, I spent most of my time in wine divisions. I got to know them all—from New World labels to the European vintages, mass market, high end, and wines made right near my home in Ontario.

Wine buying is both an art and a science. It requires understanding the numbers as far as trends and the markets go and creating a roadmap based on them. It requires building relationships. It was intense—long trips and long workdays were not uncommon—but it was an amazing ride. I met with some of the largest wine producers in the world, listened to their stories and their history. I learned about their portfolios and sat in on deep conversations about trends. I travelled to some of the places you associate with great wine.

But even if my teeth will never be the same, thanks to tasting all those bold reds, my palate and my judgement definitely came out ahead. You know that magic instinct telling you something is right and urging you to move forward even if the data to support your gut instinct aren't always there? It got me. Eventually, I resigned from my wine-buyer job to follow my passion for entrepreneurship and innovation and start my own consulting business in the industry.

Then, in 2018, Canada became the second country to legalize recreational cannabis. Some would say the dark side was calling my name (although part of this book's mission is to convince you that this so-called dark side is light grey at worst), but I wanted to know more. I think I was also ready for a different direction in life, and this new world fascinated me. In 2020, I started testing the waters via Zoom lunches with people in the cannabis industry and reading everything I could get my hands on. I quickly realized I needed to immerse myself, and I took a job with one of the largest Canadian producers of recreational cannabis at the time. It was really exciting. Not only did I get to meet the pioneers of a new entrepreneurial field, leverage a career's worth of experience in different ways, and help my company grow, but I also actually got to be in on product ideation and the creation of new brands, launching more than ninety-two products and moving to the number one market share leader in Canada within a year of joining the company.

It wasn't all giggles and munchies, like you might expect (although there were some and they were great!). Working in an industry that has only been legal for a few years had its share of challenges—limited history to predict the future, stretched resources, and trying to meet the needs of a rapidly changing consumer base contributed to my in-the-weeds learning experience.

Early in this new adventure, a stunning revelation hit me. Whenever I learned something new about cannabis, my brain automatically put the information in the context of wine . . . and it made sense! Varietals are like strains. *Indica* and *sativa* each have things in common with red and white wines, respectively. A hybrid is like a rosé, the balanced middle ground of both together. There was terroir, which is how the growing environment—soil, climate, topography, etc.—influences the scent and taste of the product, and there were notes and flavours.

One of my favourite things about wine is provenance. I find that the origins of where and when a wine is from add to my enjoyment. Guess what? The same thing applies to cannabis. Knowing where strains are from, who made them, and how they are processed matters to me and makes it a more enjoyable experience. While I love a great blended wine, I prefer single varietals due to their expression of a single grape in all its glory. That's why I prefer single strain rosin and resin-based edibles and beverages that express the strains the best.

When my family and friends began coming to me with questions about cannabis, I answered them using the basics of wine that I knew they already understood, and they loved it.

And that was the (ahem) seed of this book.

When I was growing up, wine was synonymous with celebration, class, and sophistication. My priests drank it as a key element of communion. In fact, in February 2024, the Pope himself declared wine a "gift from God."[1] My parents bought fancy bottles for special occasions. And, of course, each New Year featured a midnight Champagne toast, expressing a hope of epic things to come.

Weed, on the other hand, was a pineapple express train straight to Hell. That's what parents and teachers told me, and that's what I believed. In Canada, we had been just as well trained to "just say no" as our American cousins.

So, while I have always been comfortable with wine, I felt weird about weed. Getting to know cannabis was a lifelong toe-dipping exercise. It took years to break through those family and social barriers, get educated, and give myself permission to choose what's best for me.

Like many people, my first experience with cannabis was at university. I was on the brink of independence. One night when I was feeling rebellious, I attended a house party. A good friend of mine took out a baggy from his jeans pocket, and we slipped out back, looking for a dark corner. I watched as he carefully cradled a rolling paper, then sprinkled the bag's contents in the fold . . . and, impossibly, he rolled it with one hand. One hand! He finished off by giving it a lick and a twist.

He seemed so confident and so chill. Meanwhile, my internal voice wouldn't shut up. It had me casually glancing around to make sure that no cop was going to jump out of a nearby bush because—let's be clear—I would NOT do well in prison. When the joint was passed to me, that voice was saying, "Jackie, don't cough. And for Pete's sake, try to do something cool when you exhale." I imagined myself puffing out tendrils like a design in the foam on top of a latte.

Let's just say that's not how it went down. I know we've all heard this before, but I'm certain I didn't inhale . . . much. There might have been coughing. Lots of coughing. There was certainly embarrassment. And there was guilt. So much guilt. I went back to my berry-flavoured wine cooler ASAP. I never really got past those feelings, either, not as a young adult. I couldn't get comfortable using weed after that first experience. Yeah, I would occasionally take a drag if a joint was passed to me, but I preferred the legal pleasure of a glass of wine. That remained true long after I graduated and entered the professional world.

I developed a beautiful relationship with wine. Give me a good friend and a bottle of Napa cab on a Friday night, and believe me, major world issues will be solved. I nurtured a great group of friends who also enjoy a great glass of wine. These are authentic, health-conscious, happy people with successful careers.

And almost every one of them smokes or consumes weed. Because of my profession, it seemed natural to them that wine would be my substance of choice at social events. And it was! But, in all honesty, it was also a shield. If I had a glass in my hand, I didn't have to accept the joint when it was passed around. And that was good because even though I admired and respected these people, I still felt uncomfortable about weed. They would swear by cannabis, describing how it helped reduce anxiety, ease pain, create focus, or take sex to the next level. I would try to argue that a glass of wine might do the same trick. Or maybe a bottle. Or perhaps an entire winery's worth.

Then, around the same time that calorie and carb counting became a bigger part of my life, and while Canada was preparing to legalize recreational cannabis, I attended another house party. I was a wiser, more sophisticated Jackie than that undergrad hiding in a dark corner of some kid's yard. The hostess brought out a beautiful, handcrafted box, complete with a custom antique-looking lock and key. She held it with care and respect, opening it to display the most impressive collection of cannabis and accessories that you've ever seen. There were little glass jars with cork tops, each one containing a unique strain of cannabis. She told us the history and potential effects behind each one. She explained the profile and shared her own experiences with all the guests.

It was exactly how I present wine at my dinner parties. It was exactly the way I go about selecting a beautiful bottle of vintage wine from a cellar where it has been carefully stored at just the right temperature. It was exactly the way I handle each presentation, pouring that wine into a stunning decanter, and matching it to the right glass before serving it to my friends. It was like a lightning bolt straight to my brain.

In that moment, a major perspective shift occurred for me. I decided it was time for me to take another look at this plant to see if we couldn't rekindle the relationship on a better footing.

Feeling brave and liberated, I went to a dispensary and bought a pre-rolled joint. I'm so grateful for pre-rolls because for the life of me I still can't roll a proper joint, let alone do it one-handed. I brought it back to my cottage and sat looking closely at it as I sat out on the dock. That evening, all those years of wine experience kicked in.

I noticed how the joint was assembled. I smelled it carefully. At last, I sparked up and inhaled very slowly. I let myself cough a little. Don't get me wrong—that internal teenage voice was still there, and she was going crazy. *Is this safe? Whatever happened to just saying no, Jackie? Am I going to be that mom who finally got pushed over the edge and turned to pot?* Then my confident adult voice spoke up. *Jackie, you are a courageous and empowered woman. YOU get to decide whether this plant has a place in your life or not. Period.*

And I experienced a revelation.

No, it wasn't a weed-inspired vision or epiphany, though the effects were nice. It was the full realization that instead of being in an uncharted territory, I was on very familiar ground. You could approach cannabis just like wine! It's like they are cousins. What I love about wine is the passion in the process—the care that goes into the cultivation of grapes, the terroir, the history, the stories of the vineyards. I realized that if you took out the noise and the propaganda surrounding the cannabis plant, the same things apply.

As a wine lover and industry professional, I couldn't wait to explore those synergies.

This book is for the wine lover who is curious about cannabis, if perhaps a little apprehensive. My aim is to help you *chill* about all things cannabis. The information you'll find here comes from my years of experience in the wine industry, as well as my more recent professional involvement with cannabis product development and distribution.

I was one of several beverage alcohol experts who saw the innovation happening in this new space, got excited, and made a job transition, in my case, to one of Canada's largest licensed cannabis producers. Since making the switch, I've had more fun at work than I'd had in years, and I'm dying to share everything I've learned with anyone who has ever shared my sense of apprehension and confusion about this beautiful plant.

If what you're looking for is a manifesto for the stoner lifestyle, full of claims about famous historical figures who smoked up (although there are many we could mention) and the laundry list of complaints and ailments that marijuana can cure, this isn't the book for you. If your upbringing and cultural experience made you unduly afraid of a plant that has a lot to offer, then this IS the book for you. Now that legalization is removing hurdles for law-abiding types, lots of people want to explore how cannabis contributes to their enjoyment of life, but just don't know where to start. Or simply want to become familiar with the concepts. If that's you, this book will get you going.

In this book, I aim to provide information and insights into the world of cannabis. However, it is important to note that laws and regulations concerning cannabis vary across countries, provinces, states, and regions. This book most certainly does not endorse or promote illegal activities related to cannabis or wine use. It is essential to be aware of personal tolerance levels and potential side effects. Use cannabis responsibly and legally, always prioritizing your safety and well-being.

First, some good news: if you're enthusiastic about wine and have taken the time to educate yourself a bit about it, you can leverage the basics to enhance your comfort with cannabis from the start. I have broken things down in a way that's meant to reflect the books you probably already have on your shelves—the beginner's guides to tasting and appreciation that we go to when we want to increase our knowledge of life's epicurean pleasures.

Chapter 1, Grape and Bud: A Family History, traces the parallel development of both plants over centuries. We will look at the *Vitis* and *cannabis* species, both of whom played important roles in *Homo sapiens* history. We will trace human interaction with both (yes, including some celebrity hook-ups) and learn about the roles they played in different cultures as civilization grew. We will also examine the factors that led to one species climbing the social ladder while the other ending up on the wrong side of the law.

Chapter 2, Anatomy of Bush and Vine, will give you a quick and easy breakdown of the biology of each plant, as well as some handy facts about plant chemistry.

Chapter 3, Ingest, Inhale, Absorb, digs into how the human body responds to these delightful chemicals.

Chapter 4, Making the Magic Happen, is everything you ever wanted to know about cannabis production but were afraid to ask. It leverages knowledge and skills you already have as a wine lover. A quick refresher on how grapes are grown and processed into wine serves as the starting point for a light-hearted lesson on how cannabis is cultivated and processed into products.

Chapter 5, The Labels They Wear (and How to Read Them), provides an illustrated guide to both wine and cannabis labelling so you can choose the right products for your interests or the occasion.

Chapter 6, Let's Go to the Dispensary, will take you to the dispensary (surprise!) and explain the process of shopping for cannabis products.

Chapter 7, Grow Your Own, is all about guiding you through the steps of growing your own weed. This book wouldn't be complete without at least putting this option on the table.

Chapter 8, Socializing with Cannabis, walks you through the basics of using cannabis in social situations, including some beginner's guidance on hosting a cannabis-inclusive meal or event in your home.

Chapter 9, Spliff Safety, breaks down for you the potential hazards of using cannabis and how to enjoy it safely.

And if you're one of those people who lives for research and dreams of being on the special cannabis edition of *Jeopardy*, there's a glossary at the end where you can find additional sources of information.

As we begin, let me say that this book is not intended to convert you from wine- to weed-lover. Despite my experimentation and my change of career, cannabis has never ousted wine from its preferential place in my life. Wine is in my soul, and nothing—nothing—will ever replace it. Instead, I hope to empower you to expand your life's experiences and broaden the field of pleasures available to you. You are in control, and ultimately you decide what has a place in your life and what doesn't.

But, if your curiosity about cannabis has been cut short by a fear of having to step into the shadows to experience it, my mission is to bring the topic out into the light so you can chill and satisfy that curiosity without shame. I can't wait to introduce you to this beautiful plant in all its Super Cheese glory.

Ready for your first puff, sip, or gummy? Well, just read on.

— 1 —

Grape and Bud: A Family History

My first experiences with alcohol were as sneaky and unauthorized as the night I first tried weed. I remember my grandfather was a real epicurean. He loved everything from chocolate to escargot to Limburger cheese (insert barf emoji here). And he convinced me to try everything at least once, except the wines, which I wasn't allowed to touch.

Once, during my eighth-grade year, he opened a sweet (off-dry in wine terms) German Riesling to share with the other grown-ups and sat it on the counter next to several other open bottles. I kept a close watch until everyone else left the room, and then dove in for a sample. Well, I grabbed the wrong bottle and ended up with a mouthful of Uncle Mike's homemade wine. Oh god, it was like vinegar and lemon juice with something vaguely floral. I'm amazed I didn't swear off alcohol for life.

But, of course, I didn't. In high school, my friends and I would take turns borrowing from our parents' liquor cabinets. Yeah, we'd make up the difference with water or tea, and think the grown-ups didn't notice, just like you might have. We would meet before whatever dance or party was about to start, pour all our stolen contributions into one big container, and start drinking. If the blended booze tasted too awful, we would add cola or orange juice. We called it swamp water (because that's what it tasted like), and we'd drink it in shifts because we were afraid we'd get buzzed after a few sips. We thought we were brilliant. I'd blush if I weren't confident that there's at least a good chance you did the same thing.

Here's the part of it which took me a long time to understand. Even though my early experiences with wine were just as illicit as my youthful cannabis adventure, and just as embarrassing, I never felt the same sense of shame and repulsion. In fact, I willingly came back to wine when I was of age and have had many great experiences. I finally got to try an amazing German Riesling, and to see Uncle Mike's wine skills steadily improve with time. I got to build a whole career out of it. It all worked out fine.

So, why on earth could I not chill about weed for so many years? Why are there so many other people like me who can laugh about their youthful indiscretions with booze while clutching a highball glass, but can't admit to smoking a joint once in anything other than a whisper? ("Mumble . . . but I didn't inhale . . . mumble.")

To answer those questions, we have to explore the origins of that fear and prejudice. To do that, we'll have to go back to prehistory, when both *Vitis* and *cannabis*—we'll consider them cousins, even though technically they are not—had great relationships with humans.

WEED AND WINE IN THE ANCIENT WORLD

The earliest evidence for human civilization goes back about 44,000 years. Our first behaviours apparently included making tools, pigments, jewellery, and—seriously, this is considered civilized—poisons.[2] We started consuming both grapes and cannabis while our species was still in hunter-gatherer mode. We figured out plant cultivation around 12,000 years ago, and both wine grapes and cannabis were among our earliest crops. The 32,000 years in between must have been a real drag for our ancestors.

There is evidence that people had access to a naturally occurring wine that collected near grape vines when the fruit fermented, burst, and then

> **Chill Fact**
>
> Cannabis is also a cousin of Humulus, the hop plant that beer makers revere.[3]

formed pools. It must have been the worst kind of plonk, more vinegar than vino (I'm looking at you, Uncle Mike), but you know humans—we'll try anything once. Or, in my case, multiple times.

As far as cannabis went, our wandering ancestors discovered that the plant fibres were useful, the seeds were edible, and the flowers were good for both pain relief and relaxation. Some genetic research suggests that the oldest prehistoric form of the plant lacked the chemical that humans find pleasurable, so it's possible that Stone Age tribes wove cloth from the fibre long before anyone thought to chew or smoke it. There's also debate about which name came first: cannabis or hemp. More on that later—for now, let's talk about civilization and cultivation.

Chill Fact

Both cannabis and Vitis likely emerged in the same region, what's now called the Caucasus mountains. That's the area between the Black Sea and the Caspian Sea, where Russia, Georgia, Azerbaijan, and Armenia come together.[4]

When humans explored and settled new territory, the cousins went with them, yet they ended up travelling in different directions. The plant that would become *Vitis vinifera*, the European wine grape, spread south and west. The earliest wineries and agricultural vineyards seem to have been in Turkey and Armenia.[5] People then carried the vines spreading over Mesopotamia and across the water to the Greek and Roman territory. The Romans, who had a taste for both wine and military conquest, established *vinifera* vines anywhere it looked like it might grow, including ancient Gaul. They may have been violent and hedonistic, but without the Romans, there might be no French or German wines. So, you know, hail Caesar!

While *Vitis* was hanging out with guys like Julius, Claudius, and Nero, hemp's ancestors moved east. *Cannabis indica*, or kush, evolved after rooting in the chilly Himalayas.[6] In the mild to hot weather of the Middle East and Africa, *Cannabis sativa* emerged. BTW, there's a third variety, *ruderalis*, but it mostly grows wild and isn't nearly as useful, so nobody talks about it much—kinda like the crazy uncle every family has but pretends they don't.

> **Chill Fact**
>
> Sativa is the strain that produces the iconic stem with five skinny, feathery leaves. Kush leaves are plumper, and each stem has seven leaves.

As humans settled into farming communities, cannabis made its way to China and India. Wherever it was cultivated, people explored cannabis's utility in crafts, medicine, and rituals. They then carried these products on trade routes to places like Egypt and Greece. Israelite priests burned cannabis on the altar in their temples[7]; ancient Egyptians put it in painkillers and pyramid caches.[8] Hemp fibre went into rope and fine, silk-like fabric made by Venetian artisans. There have even been traces of it found in Viking shipwrecks. In many places and periods, it was one of a variety of plant-based chemicals kept in the pantry. In fact, the only place that cannabis apparently didn't travel in our early history was the region that would become Britain and the United Kingdom. Those poor Brits!

What I want you to notice about these plants and their parallel history is that both crops were just . . . crops. Gifts from Mother Nature with a variety of uses. Neither *Vitis* nor cannabis was considered naughty, illicit, or a one-way ticket to the refuse pile. Sure, if you were the sort of person who spent all day imbibing a mind-altering substance, your neighbours would give you the side eye. But that was true no matter the source of your preferred high. Our prejudices against pot are mostly modern.

GREEN GODDESSES

As civilization slowly advanced, evolving from agricultural to industrial, *Vitis* and *cannabis* played different roles in different societies. A lot of it depended on how easy it was for people to get their hands on products from each plant.

One major differentiator involves access to the crop. If you lived in an area where grapevines flourished, and anyone with a plot of land could grow one's own, you could consume grape-based goods every day, hence the Romans' eagerness to try and get it to grow in as many parts of the empire as possible.

In fact, in many places, wine might have been safer than water, as the fermentation process kills bacteria. Wine or wine vinegar can also be used to clean wounds, or as a base for liquid medicines.

However, if you had no vineyards or wineries close by, you had to rely on imports from trade ships or caravans, which was risky. Because storage containers were primitive, things sometimes rotted en route. A lot of goods ended up at the bottom of the ocean or the bottom of a pirate's belly. Add to that the fact that wine is labour-intensive to make, to store, and to transport. In many parts of the world, it could have been so expensive that it was a luxury only the rich could enjoy, except for celebrations like holy days, festivals, or a dignitary's wedding feast. Basically, the farther you got from where the grapes were grown, the greater the cultural perception that wine was high-class. And if you were a member of the growing Christian religion, it had the added cache of being the blood of your god.

BOTANY CAN BE A REAL B*TCH

Now we get to the second differentiator: how human knowledge influences strength and dosing. Vintners began to dial in the science of wine making even before our species really understood what chemistry was or how it worked. Could an ancient Roman have told you that it was the fruit sugars that were responsible for that whole fermentation-and-transformation thing? No. But they observed that as fruit started to decompose and break down, it made interesting by-products. With the right containers and a little effort, wine or vinegar makers could influence how those by-products behaved. They observed that certain grapes had certain flavour profiles, and that different techniques could make the wine stronger and have a more intoxicating effect. The people of many early cultures understood that some beverages hit harder and faster. They also knew that effect could be reduced by mixing the beverage with other liquids, such as water.

Arabic scientists figured out how to extract the active ingredient—what we call ethyl alcohol—from wine by about 850 CE. So, we humans had a pretty good idea what we were dealing with and how to work with it from early in the history of civilization.

And we kept working to dial it in, too. Precise systems of measuring alcohol by volume developed in the 1800s, with the United Kingdom, United States, and France each developing its own chemical techniques. That means that by the start of the modern age, when *V. vinifera* beverages were becoming more globally available (at least to the upper classes), a drinker could have a pretty good idea how potent his or her burgundy, port, and brandy were.

Chill Fact

England developed the first test of alcohol strength in the 1500s. It was pretty basic. You dropped a gun pellet from one of those new-fangled rifles in the liquid, took it out, and tried to light the gunpowder inside it. If the ball caught fire, that was a high alcohol beverage.[9]

With *Cannabis indica* and *sativa*, it wasn't that straightforward. Yes, growers have long understood that breeding and cultivation techniques can influence the character of their crops. That was as true for cannabis as for grains or grapes. But Mother Nature also had a say, and factors like the weather, pests, and simple genetic expression have an impact on how the buds of a plant turn out. Sometimes even two plants from the same crop can have chemical variations, just like one tomato plant in your garden might flourish while another gives almost no fruit.

More importantly, science didn't pinpoint the active ingredient that gets us to Happy Town until—get this—1964. Tetrahydrocannabinol (THC) is more complex than ethyl alcohol, and before the twentieth century, humans didn't have the skills or tools to isolate it. The closest we came was centuries ago, with a technique to concentrate the resin that grew on cannabis flowers and enhance its potency. The result was hashish. More potent, yeah, but still not very precise.

What does that mean? While humans have valued the medicinal properties of cannabis since our species started to ingest it, we didn't really know how it worked as it was long before we had the chemistry to prove what was happening. If you have experimented with cannabis in the past, you may already see where I'm going with this. You might remember that you could share a joint or a brownie with a friend one night and feel almost nothing. Then, the next Saturday, you could do the same exact thing and end up singing love songs to your hairbrush for the next six hours. That's likely because your weed guy was getting his product from different growers or sources and there was the lack of emulsion advancement at the time for proper infusements. (I'm happy to say that this is far from the case today!) Earlier societies could control that, to a certain degree, if you lived in a village that grew its own cannabis crops, or traded selectively with those who did. But it wouldn't guarantee complete command over the plants. There were just too many factors outside of human influence to ensure that every flower from one harvest, or across harvests, would be the same quality. The best you could do is try it out yourself, and then tell the neighbour, "Look out, Ogg, this batch will really mess you up." Whether you're talking about grapes or cannabis buds, each one is unique. As a result, you can have a controlled space growing the same varietal or strain, yet there will be chemical variances from one to another. Although we may have the same parents, grow up in the same town, and live in the same house, we are not the exact same as our siblings.

This became more of a problem as cannabis spread as a global product. Whether the end use was evening prayers, soothing menstrual cramps, or chilling with friends, neither the producer nor the user could really be sure how strong the dose might be. When mixing elixirs and tinctures, doctors or pharmacists could only make their best guess, especially if they weren't getting their ingredients from the same producer every time.

At the time, cannabis was also just one of a variety of psychotropic or narcotic products competing for market share in developed countries. Remember, this was WAY before you could just go get a bottle of ibuprofen from the grocery store or pull an ice pack out of the freezer. When humans had aches and pains, they turned to plants for relief. That could mean cannabis. It could also mean willow bark, poppy juice, or coca leaves. Early civilizations had been stuck with what they could grow in the fields around their village. Once international trade became a regular thing, medical practitioners and chemists had more to work with.

In the 1830s, an Irish born, Scotland-educated doctor was a professor at the medical college in Calcutta where he was studying the medical application of cannabis. Dr. O'Shaughnessy's work led him to recommend cannabis for a number of ailments: he found that cannabis could lessen pain associated with rheumatism and stop convulsions in infants, among other things. Soon cannabis was popular in England for a variety of medicinal applications.

Some of the biggest cure-alls from these early modern days would earn twentieth-century reputations as poison. Consider opium poppies and coca plants.

Poppies had long been in use for pain relief in many societies; many villages throughout Britain had their own poppy patches so they didn't have to go to town every time someone got a toothache. Opium was available in many forms: powders, tinctures, drops, pills, and so on. It could be mixed with alcohol and sold as laudanum or distilled as injectable morphine.[10] Victorian-era doctors liked that it could be measured precisely and acted quickly. They prescribed it for everybody from wounded soldiers to teething babies.

Likewise, coca leaves were being processed into a white powder that was also considered another wonder drug of the age. In liquid form, cocaine was a useful topical anaesthetic. In powder form, it could make the user feel alert and energetic. A French chemist even combined it with Bordeaux wine to make an early energy drink called Vin Mariani that was endorsed around 1860 by Pope Leo XIII. (His successor, Pope Pius X, drank it, too.) In 1886, a sweet, carbonated cocaine-laced drink hit the American market as Coca-Cola.[11]

There's a reason both opium and cocaine captured so much market share. The active ingredients in both opium poppies and coca plants are alkaloids, a kind of salt. By the 1800s, any scientist worth his or her, well, salt could precipitate salts like a boss. THC, on the other hand, is much tougher to isolate. So, while people were glad to have cannabis as another option for health and recreation, it wasn't the most reliable or effective thing on the market, so it didn't become an overnight sensation.

By 1900, it was clear that both opium and cocaine created more problems than they solved. New chemical techniques had allowed them to be refined to peak purity and efficacy, but also made it easy to form a dependency, and hard to quit. Until we really understood the dark side of opium and cocaine, they were the belles of the medical ball. In the nineteenth and twentieth centuries,

cannabis was commonly used as a medicine and was even included in the *United States Pharmacopeia*.[12] And until humans had the agricultural botany and chemistry know-how to harness the compounds in weed, cannabis herself would be just another pretty face.

Unfortunately, that face would spend most of the twentieth century on wanted posters throughout the Western world.

BAD GIRLS

So where did things go sideways? How did we get here, with one cousin a fixture of high society and the other on the wrong side of the law for a century?

To explain that, first, I need to go back and qualify a statement I made near the top of this chapter. Remember when I said that "our prejudices against pot are mostly modern"? Well, now I'd like to highlight that word, "mostly,"

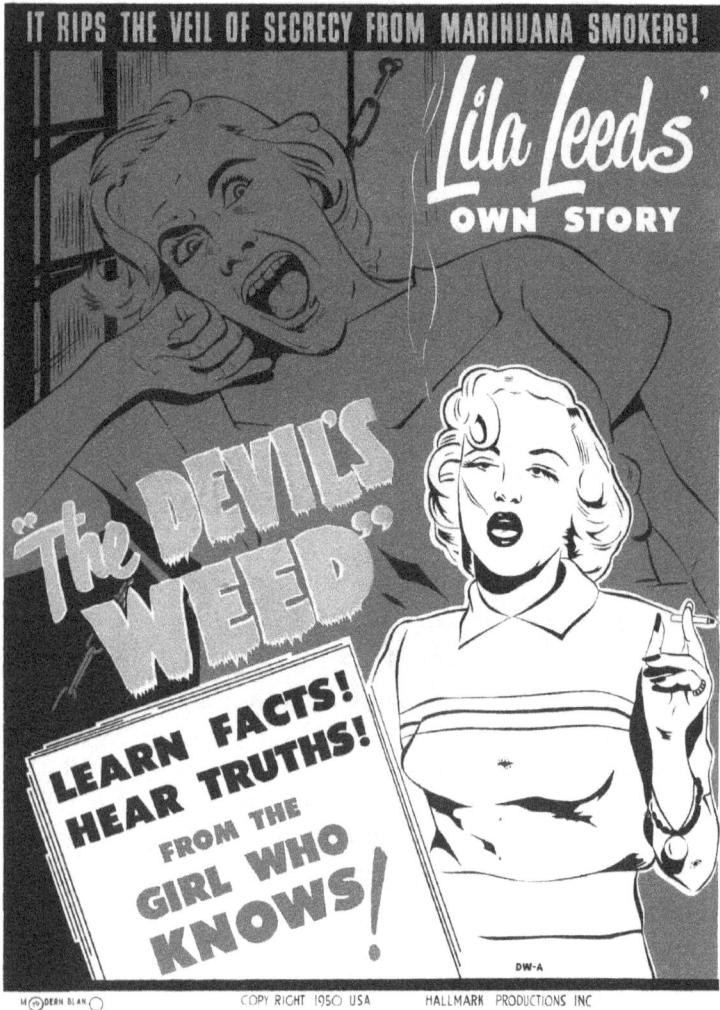

IT RIPS THE VEIL OF SECRECY FROM MARIHUANA SMOKERS!

Lila Leeds' OWN STORY

"The DEVIL'S WEED"

LEARN FACTS!
HEAR TRUTHS!
FROM THE
GIRL WHO
KNOWS!

COPY RIGHT 1950 USA   HALLMARK PRODUCTIONS INC

because some of the exceptions can help us understand how this plant came to have such a scary reputation for people like you and me. History can be a rabbit hole you fall into and never get out of, and I don't want that to happen to us. So, I'm acknowledging up front that the story is far more nuanced and complex than what you'll find in these pages (isn't it always?). For now, I'm breaking it down to three influences: church, colony, and class. With all three, it kinda comes down to us versus them.

Most religions feature the ritual use of some substance; many have been vocal in their criticism of other religions' substances, too. It's human nature to be cool with what's familiar (i.e., what my god says is ok), and totally suspicious of what's not (i.e., what your god says is not ok). Over the centuries, if one belief system became powerful in a place, it got to work trying to ban the practices of competing faiths. For example, Christian priests in the Middle Ages prohibited the use of psychedelics like mushrooms and foxglove because pagan ceremonies used them. And it was never enough for the authorities to say, "Just don't do it." They always gave a list of the evils associated with the banned substance.

Vitis has had her share of critics over the ages. Hindu, Buddhist, Jainist, and Bahá'í scriptures have all spoken out against alcohol and drunkenness. The Quran calls out wine—made with either grapes or dates—specifically as haram or forbidden. Taoism condemned all intoxicants as early as the fifth century BCE. Muslim societies have always had mixed feelings about cannabis; while hashish had been popular in the Arab world for a long time, theologians couldn't agree about whether it was ok. Some sects and countries continued to embrace it, while others argued that it was an intoxicant just like alcohol, and, therefore, the Prophet wouldn't have approved.

So, the precedent was there. That means that, in the early twentieth century, as cannabis became increasingly associated with Mexican immigration into the United States, preachers already had a them-versus-us playbook they could take with them onto the pulpit. Where it had once been a blessing, it was now the devil's weed.

Before you accuse me of blaming God(s), politics was just as big a factor, and for just as long. If you're trying to control a population, you're likely to restrict access to the things you think might initiate a rebellion or criminal behaviour—or sometimes just the stuff that they enjoy. That includes intoxicants.

Vitis has her share of experience with legal prohibition. Just a few modern examples: British missionaries pressured the colonial governments to forbid alcohol in several African colonies in the Victorian age; it was illegal in the

Faroe Islands for most of the twentieth century; the ayatollahs banned it in Iran in 1979. In most cases, local or federal authorities have been responding to pressure from religious or moral reform groups that see alcohol consumption as a source of crime, degeneracy, and moral decay.

Cannabis has plenty of history as an outlaw. Even though they were the ones to introduce *Cannabis sativa* plants to the New World, Conquest-era Spaniards spent a lot of time trying to keep native populations from consuming psychotropic varietals. The Portuguese tried over and over to stamp out use among the enslaved peoples they had brought to Brazil, many of whom carried hemp seeds with them on the Middle Passage. The British used a tax and regulated philosophy to try and control cannabis growing in India during the Raj. And that's just the tip of the iceberg.

Finally, social class has a lot to do with how a culture sees each intoxicant available to it. I explained earlier in this chapter how wine came to be associated with wealth, privilege, and power. For much of the world, it was (and still can be) an expensive import that the rich use to show off their status. In contrast, weed is something that almost anyone can grow oneself, making it more accessible. *Vitis* is the guest of honour at all the best parties; cannabis hangs out at the backyard barbecue. Is it a surprise that the instinct of the ruling class is to celebrate one and dismiss the other as common, with all the baggage that term carries?

Now that we've got the pieces of this psychological puzzle, let's try to put it all together with some help from Ryan Stoa, the author of the book *Craft Weed*. Stoa argues that the ruling class usually controls whether marijuana growing is legal or not.[13] According to Stoa, this isn't a modern thing at all, but has happened for centuries, and usually when the people with the power— whether that be religious, political, or social—are trying to crack down some perceived threat to that power. He says that the commonality between these prohibitions is inequality or fear of the unknown. The people doing the banning justify their choices by arguing the dangers of the thing they want to ban: it causes antisocial behaviour, leads to crime and violence, and threatens to destroy society.

This has happened to both *Vitis* and *cannabis* in different places at various points throughout history, and it's what has led to our attitudes today. When someone says "prohibition," you and I probably think of the same thing, the big

P "Prohibition" enacted by the Eighteenth Amendment to the US Constitution. It went into effect in January of 1920, and the "manufacture, transportation, and sale of intoxicating liquors" would remain illegal until December 1933.

In *Brave New Weed,* Dolce links anti-cannabis and anti-alcohol sentiment in the United States starting in 1913 with bans in individual states. He argues, however, that the motivation behind the restrictions differed. On the one hand, the hatred for wine expressed by temperance societies was about what they saw as the social ills caused by drink. On the other hand, the hatred for weed was about fear and suspicion of people—the immigrant populations with whom it was popular. As Mexican immigrants flowed across the border, Southwestern states began working to outlaw the "mariguano" they brought with them.

As temperance advocates persuaded lawmakers that alcohol was the greatest threat to society, it wasn't difficult for them to sweep narcotics into the same basket of evils. Remember how public opinion and the law turned against opiates and cocaine in the early twentieth century? Though *Cannabis sativa* and *indica* didn't share the ugly side effects and addictive character of poppy and coca derivatives, in the eyes of North American authorities (and of the law in an increasing number of countries), all narcotics and psychotropics should be considered the same. Whether the average Joe agreed or not, according to American law, both alcohol and cannabis were now dangerous—and therefore illegal—vices.

Consider the three temperance posters given next published in Canada during the 1910s, currently housed in the Provincial Archives of Alberta, Canada. The drivel they were talking about wine is pretty much the same as what we've all heard about cannabis during the last fifty years.

The Eighteenth Amendment, prohibition of alcohol in the United States, was repealed after thirteen years. None too soon. It was just in time for the Great Depression to hit, which meant that everybody probably needed a drink. *Vitis* was in the clear, but cannabis wasn't so lucky. Anti-immigrant sentiment grew as unemployment got worse, and weed had become firmly associated with foreigners in the minds of many. There was no scientific evidence to support that moderate cannabis use was physically harmful, addictive, or likely to cause violence or psychosis. Nevertheless, several bureaucrats were still convinced that it was as dangerous as any opiate, and they sponsored a public

GRAPES TO WINE

WATER 80%

FOOD VALUE 20%

GRAPES

WATER 80%

FOOD VALUE 20%

GRAPE JUICE

WATER 78%

ALCOHOL 17½%
FOOD VALUE 4½%

WINE

GRAPE JUICE (UNFERMENTED) IS GOOD AND WHOLESOME
Wine contains Alcohol which is a Poison

Published by The Dominion Scientific Temperance Committee

Temperance Lesson No. 2

campaign to convince Americans of that fact. We might think that the film *Reefer Madness* is hilarious, but in 1936, it terrified the public into thinking that one drag on a joint could make you permanently insane.

To the benefit of the alcoholic beverage industry, which was trying to get back on its feet after a fourteen-year hiatus and during a terrible economy, the

Bureau of Narcotics sponsored a Marijuana Tax Act that made it financially impossible for the medical community to continue using it. After the passing of the Marijuana Tax Act, it was a short leap for those same authorities to finish ruining cannabis's good name.

The funny thing was that, prior to the Feds' smear campaign, most Americans still hadn't even heard of marijuana. (This is likely because they had previously known it to be called hemp or cannabis.) According to Dolce, only about 50,000 US citizens had smoked the plant, and those who bought patent medicines and tinctures had no idea what marijuana really was or that it was the same thing as this weird weed that lawmakers were freaking out about. So their first exposure to the plant was through popular culture classics like *Reefer Madness, Marijuana: Assassin of Youth, The Devil's Weed,* and *Marijuana Girl.* No wonder they were as afraid of it as we are of fast-moving zombies.

Cannabis, a fixture in human culture from the dawn of civilization, went from being virtually unknown to *planta non grata* throughout North America in under two decades. And she stayed at the fringes, especially in the Western, English-speaking world, for decades more.

A NEW LEAF

Since you have this book in your hands, you are probably a little bit like me. Your perception of our two cousins, *Vitis* and *cannabis,* has been shaped by the three factors I just outlined. Wine is fine because it has been legal, familiar, and comfortable for your whole life. Weed, however, seems mysterious, sketchy, and maybe even dangerous.

Now that cannabis is legal in Canada and an increasing number of places in the United States, you can set aside concerns about getting into legal trouble. You don't have to go far from home to enjoy it and still stay on the safe side of the law.

It may be tougher to break out of the prison of your own mind. I'm sure that people who care about you were always warning you about that skunk-y cannabis, telling you that you should stay well away from her because she runs with a bad crowd. And that makes perfect sense, considering that your parents, mentors, and leaders had all heard the same things themselves. They had no way to know that their information was based on a fear of foreign influences among people with religious, political, and social authority who were trying hard to resist change during uncertain times.

The whole point in this history lesson is to show you that our girl cannabis has had perfectly friendly relationships with humans since they first figured out how to walk upright. In fact, she has done a lot to help us deal with some of our biggest issues from the start. We couldn't have crossed oceans without her. She gave us clothes to put on our bodies, seeds to nourish them, and buds to create relaxation and pain relief.

Thanks to advances in science, we now have a much clearer idea of how cannabis works with our bodies. It's possible to dial in our experiences with greater precision, and to avoid the dazed-and-confused phenomenon. Growers and processors can even cultivate varietals to produce particular taste and smell profiles. You can select products based on the kind of effects you'd like to enjoy or avoid.

I'm dedicated to helping you gain the same information about cannabis that you have probably already sought out in your exploration of wine. Just as knowledge enhances your pleasure as a wine lover, it can make you feel more informed about cannabis.

Naturally, I will be presenting all this material with a focus on intention and moderation. I wouldn't want you to go overboard with cannabis any more than I would wish you to get drunk on wine every night. In the next chapter, Anatomy of Bush and Vine, I will offer a comparative anatomy lesson that will help you identify *Cannabis sativa* and *indica* with as much familiarity as the grape vines that produce your favourite bottles.

— 2 —

Anatomy of Bush and Vine

As a wine lover, the more I hung out with *Vitis*, and the closer I got to her, the more I wanted to know about vino. I wanted to know where wine came from, how it was made, who made it, and what drove them. Maybe you are the same.

Even though I love to bend my friends' ears for an hour on wine-related stories, I'm going to avoid geeking out too hard on you and stick to a basic refresher on the *Vitis vinifera* plant, just enough to give you context. We will spend a little more time with *Cannabis*: *indica* and *sativa*, the plants that turn the wheels of the weed industry.

ANATOMICA *VITIS*

Wine grapes grow on a type of vine called a liana, which is a perennial plant with a woody stem and a habit of clinging to whatever it can find for support. It is deciduous, which means that it drops its leaves in the fall and grows a new set each spring. It puts out tiny, bisexual flowers (and you thought *Vitis* was a square) that mature into the juicy seed pods that we know as grapes.

Grapes, by the way, are a type of berry.[14] The berries grow in bunches that hang down below the leaves, which are harvested in late summer, fall, and, in the case of ice wines, winter.

Because grapes do not continue to ripen after they are picked, growers wait until sugar content is at its peak, and then bring in the harvest as quickly as possible. In the case of wine grapes, the fruits will then be processed into that beverage we all love.

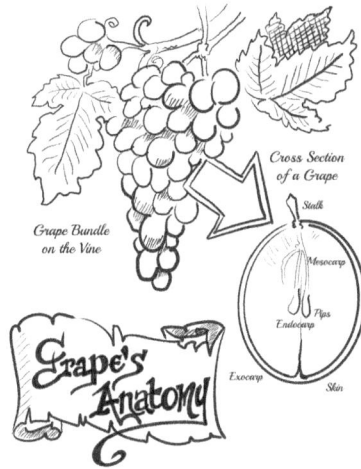

Cross Section of a Grape

Grape Bundle on the Vine

Stalk

Mesocarp

Pips

Endocarp

Exocarp

Skin

Grape's Anatomy

Chill Fact

Ice wine—my sweet, delicious favourite—harvesting temperatures must be at least –8°C, so harvest happens in winter.

ANATOMICA CANNABIS

The cannabis plant is a member of the Cannabaceae family. Another member of this family is *Humulus* (aka, hops) and shares some familiar features and traits. (Think of hops as another cousin who shows up at all the family picnics, of course in the form of beer.) Cannabis is annual, meaning that individual plants grow from seed during warm weather, cast their own seeds at maturity, and then die when the weather turns cold. The seeds turn into the next generation of plants when the next warm cycle begins.

Like the grape vine, it is wind pollinated, but unlike the *Vitis* family, for most cannabis varieties, each individual plant produces only male or female flowers.

How do you tell the difference? Well, there's a slight resemblance to human reproductive anatomy. You can see for yourself:

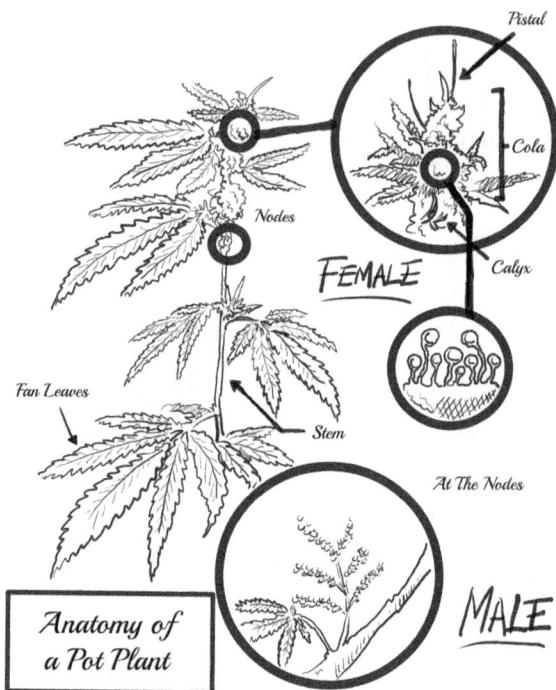

Pistal

Cola

Nodes

FEMALE

Calyx

Fan Leaves

Stem

At The Nodes

Anatomy of
a Pot Plant

MALE

Cannabis flowers are often referred to as buds. The prized cola of the plant is made up of a cluster of buds that grow tightly together on a female cannabis plant. This bushy, sticky blossom at the end of each stalk is full of tiny bulbs called trichomes. Those bulbs carry the good stuff, the chemicals that provide the high and other beneficial effects.

In addition to differences between male and female plants, *indica* and *sativa* have some easy-to-spot distinctions. *Sativa* plants are taller—a bit like a tree sapling—with leaves that

Sativa
Tall and sparse

resemble long, skinny fingers. The bud, too, is long and frizzy. *Indica* plants are shorter—think bush rather than sapling—with plump leaves that fan out like a peacock's tail. The colas have round, full pods.

These days, growers are into developing hybrid plants by combining DNA from various *indica*, *sativa*, and sometimes even *ruderalis* plants (remember the crazy uncle from Chapter 1?). The point is to try and dial in specific flavour profiles, effects, or quality of experience for the final product. If you see one of these hybrids at a farm or grow op, it might show characteristics of any or all three parent types.

Indica
Short and bushy

PLANT CHEMISTRY

If I were a tenured professor, I might go off on the whole story for both plants, from root to leaf tip. But let's be real; there are only two things you really want to know about: the grape and the bud. Those are the parts that you will consume, so let's focus on what gives each plant its most delightful properties, the phytochemicals that they each produce.

For all her sophistication, *Vitis* is a sweet, down-to-earth girl—literally. The intoxicating effect of wine comes from the conversion of the grape's natural sugars into alcohol. To make this happen, winemakers introduce yeasts into the juice. The yeasts eat the sugars, and then release carbon dioxide and ethanol as they digest. While the carbon dioxide dissipates into the air, the ethanol stays behind in the liquid that we drink.

The fermentation process is where the magic happens. It will determine the wine's colour, aroma, and flavour. Winemakers use different techniques to shape the final product. There are many chemicals—sulfites, tannins, esters, ketones, norisoprenoids, fatty acids, etc.—that influence all the things we enjoy about wine. The most important and best known of these are tannins, the phytochemicals that drive the aromas rising from your favourite glass. They determine everything from what you experience when you first put your nose in a glass to what foods pair well with a particular vintage.

All of these chemicals are important, but what about the physical effects we feel after a couple of glasses? That's all ethanol, baby.

Similar to her friend *Vitis*, cannabis has a lot of chemical compounds that impact the flavour, aroma, potency, and effects. In Chapter 1, I mentioned that it was the 1960s before science figured out what she was all about. They're still researching the reasons for her awesomeness, in fact. If you want to show your appreciation, you can send a thank you card to a team of scientists at the Weizmann Institute in Israel.[15]

Dr. Raphael Mechoulam, Dr. Yehiel Gaoni, and Dr. Haviv Edery isolated a group of chemicals that they called cannabinoids. Of the approximate 540 chemical substances that a cannabis plant produces, about 100 can be classified as cannabinoids, and these are divided into major and minor categories. The two most important major cannabinoids are:

- Tetrahydrocannabinol (THC), which is primarily responsible for the psychoactive effect of the plant
- Cannabidiol (CBD), which does not have psychotropic effects but can help with pain relief, relaxation, and anxiety reduction

Three out of the dozens of minor cannabinoids currently matter the most to us: cannabigerol (CBG), cannabinol (CBN), and cannabichromene (CBC). All of these are present in cannabis plants to some degree, but how much of each you find in a given bud can vary, based on factors like the strain, age of the plant, or maturity of the bud.

While any of these five compounds can have pleasurable or beneficial effects, many cannabis growers and researchers argue that cannabinoids are mightier as a whole than as isolated parts of the plant. They argue that the presence of multiple compounds creates an entourage effect, which produces a richer, more complex experience. Think of it as an orgy of goodness, if you want to get Greek. If that's a little too freaky for you, imagine a pop diva with her posse in tow.

Terpenes are aromatic compounds that contribute to the fragrance of everything from rosemary to lavender, and from pinecones to oranges. They also contribute to the entourage effect. By the way, many plants contain terpenes, not just members of the Cannabaceae family.

It's the terpenes that give joints the pungent tang you've picked up at rock concerts and have caused weed connoisseurs to describe their favourite buds as "dank," "skunky," or "cheesy." But before you reach for a clothes pin, let me say that cannabis does not have to stink like a boys' locker room. Like wine, many varietals can have lovely notes of lemon, pine, or other pleasing scents. We should also remember that "gasoline" and "barnyard" are commonly used wine aroma descriptors.

IT STARTS WITH A PLANT

As a fellow wine enthusiast, I'm going to assume that you already know something about how wine grapes are grown. You've probably visited a vineyard or two, taken the tour, and done some tasting. Maybe you've even tried growing your own grapes at home! In case you haven't really explored that part of *Vitis*'s life, and you'd like to find out more, I've created a list of resources that you'll find at the end of this book. That way you and I can spend our time together on cannabis, who is probably still a bit of a mystery girl.

The cannabis plant is hardy, grows well from seed in a variety of climates, is super sustainable, and matures faster than many other cash crops and trees.

First 1-2 weeks - Germination

The plant goes through five basic phases:

Next 2-3 weeks - Seedling

1. Germination
2. Seedling
3. Vegetative
4. Flowering
5. Harvesting

While both hemp and marijuana are cannabis plants, it's the amount of THC that determines how a given plant is legally classified. Less than 3 percent and you've got industrial hemp; more than 3 percent is marijuana.[16] Hemp is utilized for general products like textiles and paper, or food products like oil, milk, and protein.

The seeds themselves are nutritious as a complete protein and high in fibre and fatty acids. They are often called hemp hearts. (Ooh, my heart does love me some hemp.) And it is an incredibly sustainable crop that grows faster than trees but uses less water and requires fewer pesticides than most crops.

Marijuana has earned many nicknames, including pot, grass, and ganja. THC values can vary widely among the different strains, and they are responsible for the psychoactive high. The term marijuana is potentially problematic, considering its history in racial prejudice. It was used by politicians to highlight the foreign sound of the word, giving it a sour flavour to go along with the hatred of Mexican immigration in the 1920 and 1930s. Most industry people use the term cannabis.

Next 2-8 weeks - Vegetative

Final 6-8 weeks of growth - Flowering

Buds darken in color - cut and hang the plant for Harvesting

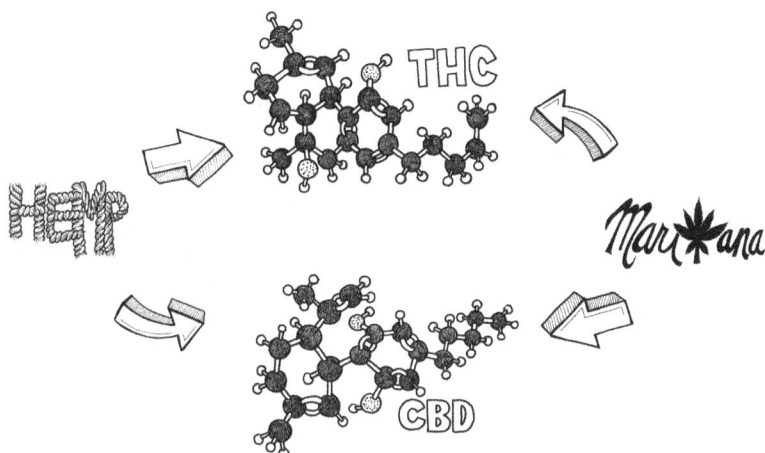

When the plant is harvested will depend on how the plant will be used. If its fibres are to be processed for cloth, paper, rope, etc., the whole plant will be cut down before the flowers are mature enough to produce seed.[17] If the goal is an edible product like seed or oil, the flowers will be allowed to mature until the seeds start to shatter, or drop from the plant.

Chill Fact

In 1941, Henry Ford debuted a car made from hemp fibre, and that ran on a hemp- and vegetable oil-based fuel. The fibres used in the body frame were ten times stronger than steel.[18]

For the high-THC cannabis plant known as marijuana, the kind we humans consume for medical or recreational purposes, cultivation has gotten seriously high tech. With wine, much of the manipulation happens after the grapes have been harvested and the vintner exposes the juice to elements that impact the flavour and alcohol content. With cannabis, most of that process happens while the plant is still growing the buds. Curing methods and time also significantly impact the end results.

While cannabis bushes can be grown outdoors in a traditional farm setting, many modern growers prefer to use greenhouses or indoor growing operations.[19] This gives the grower better control over the plants, as light types and levels, water, temperature, and other critical elements can be adjusted. It helps mediate those x-factors we talked about, those unknown variables that can influence the quality of the buds, the level of THC and other chemicals, as well as the flavour and effects of the final product.

Good growers are a mix of botanists, chemists, and alchemists. They understand how different strains have different cannabinoids and terpenes. They use breeding techniques to produce plants that manifest chemical combinations intended to give the user a specific experience—scent and flavour profile, strength, and biological reactions in the user's body. They try to enhance this experience by controlling the plant's environment in a way that encourages high-quality buds. And, because they have to think about ROI just like any other business owner, they work to maximize the yield of each plant in the grow operation before it ages out of production.

Cannabis Species Identification

Sativa

Appearance:
- Long, thin, and narrow leaves
- Light green colour
- Buds are often tall and skinny
- Plant can be 8–15 feet tall
- Often has higher THC levels than *indica* and lower CBD levels

Common claimed effects:
- Creative
- Sociable/cheerful
- Focused
- Happy/giggly
- Alert

Often used for:
- Better focus
- Easing headaches
- Decreasing depression symptoms

- Combating appetite loss
- Increasing energy

Indica

Appearance:
- Wide, thick leaves
- Dark green colour
- Buds are dense and plump
- Plant can be 2–6 feet tall
- Can often have lower THC and higher CBD levels versus *sativa*

Common claimed effects:
- Relaxing
- Calming
- Mellowing
- Causes sleepiness

Often used for:
- Reducing anxiety
- Easing insomnia symptoms
- Relieving body pain
- Relaxing and unwinding

Hybrid

Appearance:
- Cross of *sativa* and *indica*
- Sometimes formed with three or more strains
- Often expressed as *sativa* dominant, *indica* dominant or equal combination of the two

Common claimed effects:
- Depends on the combination of parent strains used

Often used for:
- A balanced high that offers light relaxation and a little focus

Ruderalis

Appearance:

- Fewer leaves, fibrous stems
- Smaller than other species and typically grows less than 2 feet tall
- Low THC content and relatively high CBD
- Grows in the wild

Common claimed effects:

- Not applicable—rarely used for consumption

Often used for:

- Breeders, due to autoflowering and hardy growing genetics

NEXT COMES THE HARVEST

If you listen closely while on a vineyard tour, someone is bound to ask, "How do you know when the grapes are ready to pick?" It comes down to a handful of physical characteristics: colour, firmness, sweetness, acidity, and ripeness. The vintner knows when the grape is right for the wine they want to make.

The cannabis grower also relies on a handful of physical factors, this time centred on two parts of the flower: the pistil and the trichome. The cannabis flower isn't soft, like a rose or daffodil; however, the beauty lies in its natural variance and details. Cannabis comes in various shapes, sizes, and vibrant colours from variations of green to purples and blues. The pistils are the long, skinny parts that stick out like cow licks. When they first appear, they are tender and white, but as they mature, they darken to a rusty colour. Trichomes—the resin glands—look like itty bitty rain drops. They start out clear, and then turn milky. If left alone too long, they get overripe and become an amber brown, which is kind of like slightly overcooking your steak. You can still consume it, but it won't be at its best. So, the grower looks for flowers with a nice green leaf; a supple, orange-brown pistil; and a full crop of milky trichomes with a few amber ones here and there. The plant will probably have a very pungent smell, too!

When the fruits or flowers are ripe, the next step is to remove them from the plant. In the case of both grapevines and cannabis bushes, premium and small batch producers will often do this by hand to avoid injuring the plant. Large mainstream operations will often use machines—with the common goal of maximizing the quantity and quality each plant offers. With a pair of shears or other cutting tool, growers cut each bunch of grapes or buds free. They will likely sterilize their tools frequently to avoid contamination between plants, in the event that one or more has developed a disease or parasite.

That said, sometimes a cannabis grower may decide to harvest the whole bush at once. Unlike *Vitis vinifera*, which is a perennial that can live for decades, all cannabis varieties are annuals lasting a single season. The children of *Vitis* never seem to age (lucky ladies!). Cannabis's daughters are more like the rest of us, and their youth is fleeting.

If the grower does harvest the whole bush, the plant will be cut at the base or uprooted, and then hung to dry. The buds will be cut after the plant has cured. This method is called hand drying and is considered one of the best methods to preserve the trichomes.

IT'S BOTANY, BABY

So, what's the big takeaway from all this science-y stuff? When you break it down, *Vitis* and *cannabis* are two of a gazillion species of plants that humans have and do consume. I hope that looking at how they function chemically, at the very base level, has begun to satisfy your chemistry curiosity.

My goal has been to take the facts about these substances out of the high school science class, demystify the whole thing, and make the plant biology and chemistry parts a little approachable and easier to understand. Also, I feel more empowered—and more likely to enjoy myself—whenever I up my knowledge about my favourite recreational substances. I want to offer you the same joy of seizing knowledge as power.

But before you can really level up from cognoscenti to connoisseur, we must dive into a little human biology.

— 3 —

Ingest, Inhale, Absorb

WHO'S KIDDING WHO? ONE OF THE MAIN REASONS BOTH WINE AND weed are so popular is because of the effect that ingesting them has on our bodies and brains. But what's the biological process that brings us the blessed buzz?

ANATOMICA *HOMO SAPIENS*

Our anatomy contributes to how we ingest, process, and feel the effects of the phytochemicals from both grape and bud. Let's start with *Vitis*.

Wine and the ethyl alcohol it carries enter the body via one major method: ingestion. We put the wine in the glass and the glass to the lips. Then the wine goes in the mouth, and we swallow. From there, it travels down the esophagus into the stomach, and then through the rest of the digestive system.

Ethanol interacts with the body by getting into the bloodstream. From the moment you draw liquid into your mouth, tiny amounts of the chemicals it contains enter vessels through the lining of the digestive system. The stomach and liver start producing enzymes to metabolize ethanol and convert it into something less potent. But it can't do that very fast, so what the body can't immediately convert goes on moving through the bloodstream.

As it travels, it causes muscles and blood vessels to relax. It slows the transmission of impulses between brain cells, as well as the production of certain hormones. The vascular system sheds tiny bits of alcohol via the skin, breath, and urine, but the majority stays in the bloodstream until the liver can process it.

As a lover of wine, you probably already know what that means. Sip on a glass over the course of an hour or so, and you'll likely enjoy physical sensations of warmth and relaxation. You can appreciate the beautiful mouthfeel, the delightful aromas, and the rich taste. And you can get into bed at the end of the night without the whole room spinning. But if you gulp down too much too fast—well, you know what follows. Too much of any good thing can sour the experience, so you and I have learned the wisdom of enjoying everything in moderation, right?

Unlike wine, cannabis and the cannabinoids it carries can enter the body via a variety of methods: inhalation, ingestion, sublingual dosing, or topical application. In other words, you can smoke it, eat it, drink it, drop it under your tongue, or rub it in. You can bathe in it, too!

Cannabis enters the bloodstream by way of the liver during ingestion. With inhalation, it doesn't take cannabinoids long to reach the central nervous system. Smoke or vapour carry molecules into the lungs, where the cells already receive and absorb molecules like oxygen quickly, usually within minutes. Think of it like taking the expressway, except not during rush hour. This is the method of ingestion that offers the highest rate of absorption, and it is what we most commonly associate with consuming cannabis.

In all the other methods, the compounds access the nervous system via a less direct route, so the effects take longer to kick in and may not be as potent as with inhalation.

Ingestion involves edibles and beverages. There may be the widest variety of products here, ranging from gummies to baked goods to sodas and cannabis-infused beverages. As with wine, the chemicals get into the tissues through the lining of the mouth, esophagus, stomach, and intestines. That takes a bit longer, and less of the chemical content may reach the

Chill Fact

Cannabis bath bombs are an increasingly popular dispensary product.

receptors. That can mean a slower-acting, milder effect.

Sublingual dosing refers to putting a cannabis-infused product, a tincture, under the tongue. This may mean dripping a concentrated extract from a dropper. Or it could be a tablet or strip that dissolves slowly. Some of it gets swallowed, and some absorbed by the mucous membranes in the mouth. The effect is usually faster and more intense than that of edibles or beverages, but less so than that of inhalation.

GUMMIES

Topical application refers to rubbing a preparation such as a cream or oil on the skin. Very few people do this to achieve a euphoric state or high, but it is a common delivery system if you're looking for pain or inflammation relief without the comfortably numb effect.

OH, THOSE CANNABINOIDS

While the methods you can use with cannabis play a large role in the nature of the effect, we also need to take a look at the main varieties of cannabinoids that also dictate the experience you can expect.

Tetrahydrocannabinol (THC) is a psychoactive cannabinoid often known for producing a high effect and sensation. It is often used for pain relief, nausea, sleep improvement, and as an appetite stimulant.

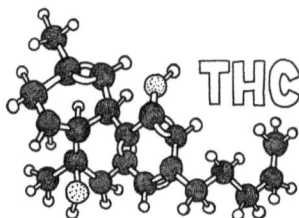

Popular THC Strains for Beginners

- Blue Dream
- Blueberry
- Jack Herer

Cannabidiol (CBD) is a non-psychoactive cannabinoid, meaning that

it does not get you high. It is most often used for pain relief, inflammation, anxiety, nausea, and migraines.

Popular CBD Strains

- Harlequin
- Green Goddess
- Charlotte's Web

There are also a few popular minor cannabinoids:

- Cannabigerol (CBG)
- Cannabinol (CBN)
- Cannabichromene (CBC)

Both CBG and CBC are non-psychoactive, whereas CBN, from my personal experience, is. CBG can however provide a boost to the bliss molecule. Dr. Mechoulam, the godfather of cannabis research, said "anandamide" is the Sanskrit word for bliss. This molecule is the endocannabinoid your body makes that mimics THC, hence his naming of it as anandamide. THC is the phyto (plant) version of anandamide.

CBG may be helpful in treating chronic pain, neurological disorders, and multiple sclerosis. Though there are currently no definitive studies. CBN may be helpful in treating insomnia or as a sleep aid. And CBC may be helpful in reducing anxiety, pain, and inflammation.

Strains Known to Have CBG

- Jack Frost
- John Snow
- Silver Haze

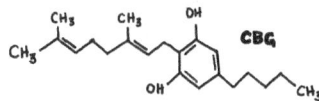

Strains Known to Have CBN

- Blackberry
- Animal Cookie
- Purple Cadillac

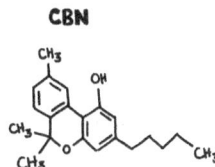

Strains Known to Have CBC

CBC

- Charlotte's Web
- Maui Dream
- Pineapple Express

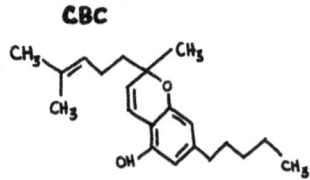

Your body actually produces its own type of cannabinoids: endocannabinoids.[20] The endocannabinoid system, or ECS, communicates with cells, and we are continuing to learn more about how it contributes to human functions and processes like sleep, appetite, emotional states, and injury response. The cannabinoids in the plant can access the same receptors in your system as the chemicals your body produces on its own. Cool, right?

There is a lot that science still doesn't understand about the ECS, our cannabinoid receptors, and how both human- and plant-produced chemicals create the effects that they do.

In order to utilize those lovely cannabinoids, there is another step required. In the same way that *Vitis* needs some extra help from yeast to ferment, cannabis requires decarboxylation, which is a chemical reaction removing a carboxyl group from the carbon chain and releasing carbon dioxide, in order to activate the compounds within the plants. Decarboxylation converts the non-intoxicating Tetrahydrocannabinolic acid (THCA) into psychoactive THC through adding heat (that's why we have to light a match or lighter when smoking a joint). With an edible, that process has already occurred during preparation. Similarly, cannabidiolic acid (CBDA) is converted into CBD with the potential therapeutic effects it offers.

From now on, whether you sip, toke, chew, rub, or rule the option of cannabis out of your life completely, you can do it knowing how the chemicals work. You'll be better prepared to select the method and make the decision that's right for you in the moment. Hey, what happens between you and the cousins, cannabis and *Vitis*, stays between you and them.

— 4 —

Making the Magic Happen

THIS CHAPTER CONCENTRATES ON EVERYTHING YOU'VE ALWAYS WANTED TO know about cannabis production but were afraid to ask.

So far, we have spent a lot of time talking about how *Vitis* and *cannabis* differ—and there are some obvious and important distinctions. Our cousins are alike in one important way, however, and that relates to how the plants turn into the products we enjoy.

People tend to assume that the journey from plant to finished product is a short, simple one. If you have thought that yourself, I'm not judging you. It does seem like it should be straightforward. You plant a vine and give it some water. Grapes grow, you pick 'em, you stomp on 'em (a la Lucy Ricardo), and you put 'em in a barrel. A few months later? Voila, wine!

And cannabis is even simpler, right? Plant a bush and give it some water. Buds grow, you pick 'em, you dry 'em, and put 'em in a bag. Then you stick 'em in your pipe (or bong or rolling paper) and you smoke 'em. Voila, pot!

I'm here to tell you—as someone who has spent time in both the wine and the cannabis industries—that there's a lot more going on than that.

GRAPES TO A GOOD PINOT GRIGIO

Most wine from grapes goes through the same basic process, which you likely already know.

The vintner has freedom to play within this system, and their choices will affect colour, smell, taste, and alcohol by volume (ABV), but the overall progression is almost always the same. Grapes become juice. Juice goes through fermentation, and then ageing. The finished liquid goes first into bottles and then into your belly (preferably via a glass, we're not cave dwellers anymore). It's a straightforward journey.

Cannabis walks a similar path with *Vitis* on this: seed, vegetative state, flowering state, harvest, dry, cure, and package. Drying and curing are replaced by fermenting and ageing in the case of wine.

TO PUFF OR NOT TO PUFF

Always the question at the forefront of cannabis enjoyment: Do you want to inhale? Or eat? Of course, each option comes with its benefits and drawbacks. This section will attempt to explain the methods of consumption to help you determine what fits your style. Choosing your methods and strains should align with your preferences and desired effects. As always, start low and go slow and give yourself time to wait for the effects to kick in before further consumption.

Smoke inhalation occurs when smoke enters the lungs before absorbing into the bloodstream. Dried flower, concentrates, and hash are commonly consumed through smoke inhalation methods.

Now things are going to get incredibly geeky. You are welcome to skim this, skip this, or dig deep, depending on what style of human you are. It's possible that you find the details to be the hottest part of the process, and if that's the case, this section is for you! But if you simply want to stay and learn about the many consumption methods, strap in!

Step 1 - Harvesting Grapes

Step 2 -
Extracting Juice

Step 3 - Fermentation

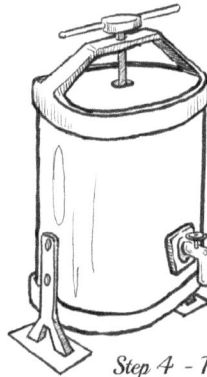

Step 4 - Pressure

Step 5 - Filtration

Step 6 - Aging & Bottling

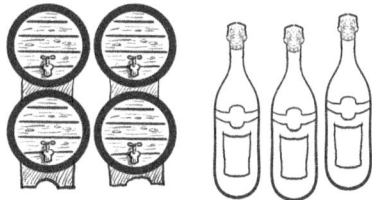

PUFFING

Rolling Papers

Rolling papers are used to make joints (dried cannabis rolled in paper). Pre-rolls are joints already rolled for you. Blunts are made by rolling cannabis in cigar paper made from the tobacco plant and contain nicotine.

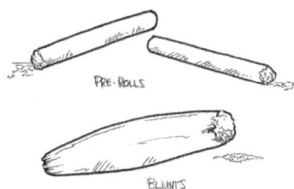

Hand Pipes

Pipes are primarily designed for dried cannabis and are often decorated with some artistic flair. They trap smoke produced from burning cannabis that is then inhaled.

Water Pipes and Bongs

Bongs and bubblers incorporate water to the hand pipe process to filter and cool the smoke before inhalation.

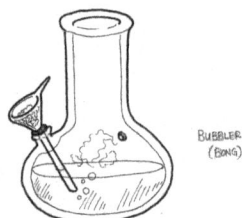

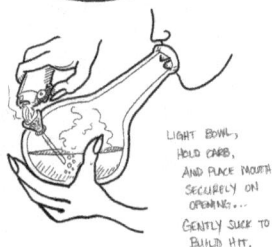

Vapourizers

Vapourizers heat up cannabis to a high enough temperature to extract THC, CBD, and other cannabinoids. They produce a vapour in the air that is inhaled. They can be used for dried flower, hash, and concentrates such as shatter, oil, and wax.

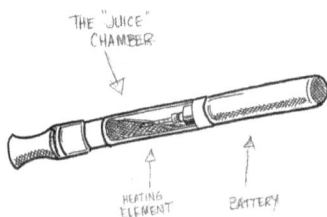

PRE-ROLLS

BLUNTS

RESONATING CHAMBER

PIPES

METAL

SCREEN

GLASS

CARB

BUBBLER (BONG)

LIGHT BOWL, HOLD CARB, AND PLACE MOUTH SECURELY ON OPENING... GENTLY SUCK TO BUILD HIT.

THE "JUICE" CHAMBER

HEATING ELEMENT   BATTERY

Dab Rig

Dabbing is specifically designed for concentrates such as oil, shatter, and wax. Once the concentrate is placed on a heated surface, called a dab rig, a vapour is produced. It should be inhaled slowly through the mouthpiece after it has moved through a water chamber.

APPLY DAB HERE

MUNCHING

On the other hand, edibles, drinks, and capsules are ingested through your digestive tract before entering the bloodstream. Tinctures are consumed orally; however, they are placed under your tongue sublingually. They do not require digestion to start working as they are immediately absorbed into the bloodstream. Topicals are cannabis products that are absorbed through the skin. Some common options are given next.

Edibles

These include gummies, beverages, chocolates, and brownies produced with cannabis, and all are consumed orally.

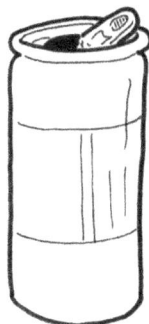

BEVERAGE

Capsules

These allow for precise dosing by orally swallowing a capsule filled with cannabis extract or oil.

CAPSULES

Tinctures

Tinctures contain a liquid extract made by soaking the cannabis flowers in a solvent like alcohol or glycerin and are often consumed sublingually, under your tongue. They can be added to food and beverages, and some are designed for topical application.

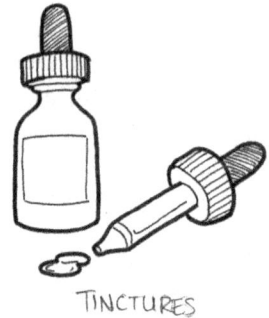

TINCTURES

Topicals

Topicals are applied directly to the skin. They are often used to target pain relief in a specific location. Bath balms, body oils, and lotions are popular topical formats and are commonly used for targeted pain relief for soreness and inflammation.

TOPICALS

Others

These include patches, sprays, sublingual strips, and suppositories.

CREATING CONCENTRATES IN ORDER TO CONCENTRATE

Cannabis concentrates, extracts, and oils are all forms of concentrated cannabis and often have higher levels of cannabinoids versus dried flower. They are generally made by extracting the desirable compounds from the rest of the cannabis plant material. There are many different extraction methods used to make them, resulting in various styles of end products. They can be broken into two categories: solventless and solvent based.

Solvent-based extracts are made with solvents such as ethanol, butane, or CO_2 in the production method while solventless extracts use heat and pressure as an alternative. They can all have very high levels of potency and regulation, which makes understanding the dosing very important.

SOLVENTLESS CONCENTRATES

Hash is a classic concentrate that comes in various forms such as the ones detailed below. It's made by separating the trichomes from the rest of the plant matter through mechanical methods like rubbing, pressing, and sifting. The resin is then formed into small blocks, cakes, or pucks, and is traditionally smoked in a joint, pipe, or bong. It can also be vapourized, dabbed, or added as an ingredient to edibles.

Hash Rosin/Live Rosin

Hash rosin/live rosin appears as a translucent amber substance that can be sticky and pliable. It's produced by applying pressure and low heat to hash and collecting the extruded resin or oil. This process ensures that cannabinoids and terpenes remain after they are extracted without the use of solvents. Hash rosin/live rosin can be dabbed, vapourized, and added to flowers and edibles. It can also be found in vape pens specifically designed for rosin.

HASH ROSIN

Bubble Hash

Bubble hash appears as a powdery, granular substance that often ranges in colour from beige to dark brown or green. It is created by soaking cannabis in ice water, making the trichomes brittle and easier to fall off. After some agitation, it moves through layered filtration bags. The stirring of the ice and buds separates the trichomes from the rest of the plant material. The trichomes and resin are dried and pressed into hash or rosin for use. This hash is often smoked in a pipe or joint, or used in vapourizers and can be used as an ingredient in edibles.

BUBBLE HASH

Dry Ice Hash

Dry ice hash is light to medium brown in appearance with a granular clumpy texture. And it is made in a similar process as bubble hash; however, dry ice replaces the use of water. It is made by

DRY ICE HASH

placing the cannabis flower in a container with dry ice, causing the trichomes to become brittle and separate easily. The plant material is then agitated and filtered to collect the trichomes. Unlike bubble hash, the drying process is not required in this process. Again, it is often smoked in a pipe or joint or used in vapourizers and can be used as an ingredient in edibles.

Kief (Dry-Sift)

Kief is a fine powdery baking powder–like substance that is light to dark green in colour. It is produced by sepa-

DRY SIFT (KIEF)

rating the trichomes glands from dried cannabis buds from the rest of the plant material by using filtering screens or specialized grinders. The powder-like substance that remains after the filtering can then be pressed into dry-sift rosin. Kief can be added to dried flower in a joint or added as an ingredient in edibles.

SOLVENT-BASED CONCENTRATES

Now let's discover the processes for the most popular solvent-based concentrates.

Live Resin

Live resin is of a vibrant amber colour with a translucent appearance similar to that of honey. It is made by flash-freezing the plant immediately after harvesting. By freezing the plant material, the process

LIVE RESIN

preserves the terpenes. This results in a concentrate that has fresh aromas and flavours. Solvents are then used to extract the desired compounds.

Distillates

A distillate is a refined oil that is transparent and clear. The consistency is similar to that of a thick syrup. A distillate is created through a distillation process using solvents, which involves the refinement of cannabis oil to isolate specific cannabinoids such as THC and CBD. This makes it versatile; however, it can result in the loss of the flowers' original terpenes and flavours. It can be used in many ways such as dabbing, vapourizing, adding to edibles and drinks, and taken sublingually.

BUTANE HASH OIL (BHO)

BHO can have a variety of textures and colours. Typically, it's amber to gold in colour and can have a soft buttery to a hard glass texture. BHO is produced by passing liquid butane through a system containing dried cannabis, which dissolves the cannabinoids and other compounds. The remaining solution is then purged of any remaining solvents, leaving behind the BHO. It is often consumed through dabbing, vaping or vape pens, or used as an ingredient in edibles and topicals.

The concentrates given next all use BHO as a part of their extraction process. Temperature changes, agitation methods, and curing times result in the unique expressions detailed next.

Wax

Wax has a waxy and sticky texture that is usually yellow in colour. It is made by purging BHO at varying temperatures and by agitating the oil during the extraction process.

Crumble

Crumble looks like dry and crumbled cheese. It is made using extraction techniques similar to those used for wax; however, it is cured longer to achieve a drier texture.

CRUMBLE

Budder

Having a creamy and buttery appearance with a smooth and malleable texture, budder is produced by purging BHO at a high temperature and whipping it during the extraction process.

BUDDER

Shatter

Shatter appears as thin glass-like sheets, usually amber in colour with a hard brittle texture. It is made by removing any residual solvents from the concentrate (known as purging) at a temperature lower than that used for budder, resulting in a more translucent concentrate.

SHATTER

The fact is, many people (including myself) primarily stick with the comfort zone. This is one of the reasons why cannabis gummies, beverages, and pre-rolls are so popular among new consumers because eating, drinking, and smoking (something already rolled for us like a cigarette) are something we're familiar with.

Hopefully this has given you all the information you need—either to choose which consumption method sounds like a fit for you or so that you have a better understanding of the lingo used to describe the different products.

— 5 —

The Labels They Wear
(and How to Read Them)

HAS GOING TO THE GROCERY STORE GOTTEN AS STRESSFUL FOR YOU AS IT HAS for me? These days, it is not enough just to wrestle a squeaky, non-ergonomic cart through the aisles, or discipline yourself to pick up the broccoli when what you really want is to reach for the chips and salsa. Nope. Now you've got to pick up every product and read the label. Calories. High-fructose corn syrup. Gluten. Salt. When did buying food become such a high-alert activity? I know when I get home, I'm ready to reach for a nice, relaxing glass of wine, a cannabis beverage, or a calming gummy.

Oh, wait. Those have labels too.

DOUBLE STANDARDS IN THE HOUSE
OF CONTROLLED SUBSTANCES

They say that families aren't supposed to play favourites . . . but we all know they do. And if constant attention and close supervision are a sign of affection, then it's easy to tell which is the favourite of the loving governmental parents in the controlled substance family. It's cannabis for sure. They're all up in her biz. Some would call their love a little overprotective, even smothering, like the most annoying helicopter parents ever.

At first glance, this might seem unfair, but if you reflect for a moment, it makes sense. *Vitis* is the oldest cousin. She's been around the longest, and she has had time to prove that she's reliable, responsible, and pleasant to be around. She earns her keep. Wine has established a comfortable place for herself in the family and pays her own way.

Cannabis, however, just got released from a long prison stint, and she's still on parole. While many believe her conviction was a miscarriage of justice, it still leaves her at a disadvantage. She's got a lot to prove and will need time to find her place in society (and her place with each of us—me included!).

All of that adds up to a serious double standard in terms of packaging. It's a situation in which *Vitis* is a lot freer to express herself, as long as she obeys a few straightforward rules. Cannabis, on the other hand, has to obey a strict dress code when it comes to her label.

Shopping for wine *or* cannabis can be a little overwhelming if you don't know how to interpret the label on the package. The rest of this chapter is dedicated to demystifying all that gobbledygook. I'll start with wine (for those who have no clue what is on there, aside from the picture, but are too embarrassed to admit it), and then move on to the specifics of the labelling for various cannabis products.

In each case, understanding the packaging comes down to five vital Ws of wine and weed: who, what, where, why, and when.

READING A WINE LABEL

Wine packaging can tell a beautiful story while introducing the content to the consumer. The label can contain everything from how old the producer is to the place the wine comes from and its lineage. It can introduce you to the winemaker or share what makes the wine unique. If you pay close attention to the label, you can create a connection to the wine beyond the liquid in the bottle.

All wine labels will carry the name of the wine, which can be serious and traditional, such as Châteauneuf-du-Pape, or as playful as 19 Crimes. They also display the name of the producer. That's the *who*.

The wine labels will display the type of wine, whether single varietal or blend, and the alcohol content. These are the *what*.

The label also shows the vintage year, which is the year the grapes were harvested—aka *when*.

In addition to these basic facts, producers worldwide are also required to name any allergens, in case the user has a sensitivity to sulfites or other ingredients.

When and why may vary from wine to wine. In Europe, labels have additional requirements, including:

Back

Wine Bottle Labelling

Take note of required information for wine labels

Front

- Product category (still, sparkling, fortified, etc.)
- Country of origin
- Provenance (proof of authenticity, origin, ownership, and storage conditions)
- A generalized health warning about the risks of consuming wine
- Added sugar content, in the case of sparkling wines

In addition to these things, some labels will indicate a special designation if the wine is a reserve or limited batch. Others will showcase the vineyard from which the grapes were sourced, and still others will highlight if the wine meets special standards, such as organic or sustainability targets.

REQUIRED INFO BY CFIA & CERTIFIED BY THE
VQA

·VITAS' VINEYARDS· ← WINERY

THE "LEAD" CAN CHANGE

• NAME
• VARIETY
• REGION

Vitas' Veil

2020 → VINTAGE

→ MERLOT ← → GRAPE VARIETY

VQA | NIAGRA PENINSULA
CERTIFICATION   APPELLATION

750 ML → CAPACITY

12.5% ALC./VOL.
ALCOHOL BY VOLUME

Front

a. Brand name
b. Wine type
c. Origin
d. Vintage (optional)
e. Marketing name (optional)
f. Special designation (e.g., reserve)
g. Vineyard designation (optional)
h. Estate bottles (optional)—winery grew 100 percent of grapes
i. Alcohol by volume—ABV (±1.5%)

Back

a. Producer and bottler
b. Net content (often 750 mL/1,500 mL [no judgement here!])
c. Declaration of sulfites
d. Government warning
e. Marketing name (optional)

READING A CANNABIS PACKAGE

There's more to learn when it comes to reading the packaging on a cannabis product, both because there's a greater variety of products to choose from and because the specifics may differ depending on the state or province where you buy. No need to worry, however; you can still look for the same five Ws. Let's look at four of the major product types: dried flower, edibles, concentrates, and pre-rolls.

Dried Flower

These packages will contain the dried, cured buds picked from the plant.

Your *who* will be the brand name and the licensed producer. You will also be able to find out who grew the cannabis and how to contact them. The lot number expressed as "Lot No." identifies the precise batch the product comes from. Next, you may see the species type—whether it is *indica*, *sativa*, or a hybrid. For strain-specific products, the specific strain name will often be on the label. The weight of the product expressed in grams will round out the *what*.

Products containing multiple cannabinoids (e.g., tetrahydrocannabinol [THC] and cannabidiol [CBD]) will often have a ratio such as 1-to-1. This means that the product contains approximately equal amounts of THC and CBD. On the other hand, a ratio of 1-to-2 indicates that there is twice as much CBD as THC in the product.

The THC and CBD levels will also be shown on the label to ensure that you know exactly how much of each is in the package you buy. It gets a little confusing because there will be two different numbers:

Example: THC 1.5 mg/g (total THC 150 mg/g)

The first number, 1.5 mg/g, refers to the active THC as it exists unheated in the package. This reflects the active THC if you were going to eat the entire packaging in the state it's in (I wouldn't recommend trying that!). The second number refers to how much active THC is in the flower after heating. In almost all cases, you can find the percentage of THC by moving the decimal place one number to the left (or dividing the total THC number by 10). In the example above, it would be 15 percent THC. You can use the same easy math

Front

Viewing windows
are not available

Packaging is opaque

CBD Packaging

Important to note
Requirements for labelling

Specific liability

Back

to determine the CBD within your flower. As a general rule, for me, 0.1–10 percent is a good starting point.

You should also find a dosage or serving size recommendation, to guide you on how much to consume at one time. These are your *what*.

Your *where* and *when* will be found in the packaging date. Sometimes you may also find more specific information on how it was cultivated.

In addition to these things, you should also see any legal or safety information required by the locality where the product is being sold. In Canada and in some US states, there will be an excise stamp attached to the package that will be torn once the products are opened and indicates that the product is legal and has not been tampered with. This stamp is not required in low-THC products.

Pre-rolls

Yes, these are joints. And the label will have much in common with dried flower, as far as the brand name, strain name and type, cannabinoid levels, and dosing go. In addition, you'll find the net weight of each of the pre-rolls typically measured in grams, a list of any other ingredients, and dates for manufacture and expiration.

Figuring out your THC percentage is a little more complicated than the dried flower. Knowing there is 1,000 mg in a gram, a common 0.5-g pre-roll that has a total THC of 60 would be calculated as follows: $60/500 = 0.12$. Multiply that by 100 to get the THC content of 12 percent.

Because inhalation can involve certain health risks, the legal language section may include some warning on that form of consumption.

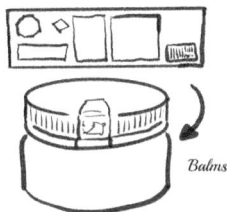

Balms

More CBD Packaging

Oils

Shorts in a Tin

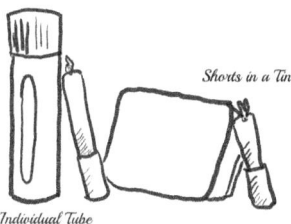

Individual Tube

Prerolls

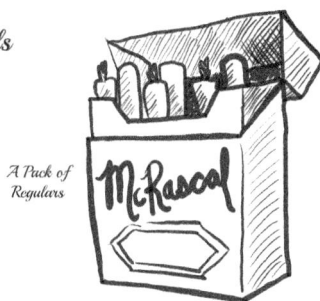

A Pack of Regulars

McRascal

Edibles

These packages will contain a food or beverage product—anything from a gummy to a soda to a cupcake—infused with a cannabis concentrate or extract.

Your *who* will be the maker of the product—cultivator or producer—and licence number assigned to them by the government.

The *what* information on the label will convey the strain name and type used to make the cannabis input emulsion, THC and CBD levels of the product, and a dosage or serving size recommendation.

CBD Gummies

Edibles

One of the unique consider-ations with edibles is the addition of the amount by unit informa-tion. If a package says it has "THC per unit 2 mg" and there are five gummies in the pack, it means the entirety of the package (all five gummies combined) has 10 mg of THC. Beverages are considered one consumable unit. As a result, the THC and CBD milligrams stated refers to the entire can or bottle and is often between 5 and 10 mg in Canada and can go much higher in certain US states, per unit.

Infused Drinks

Because these are food/beverage as well as cannabis, it will include an ingredients list and nutritional information.

You'll see an expiration date (the *when* in this case) and any storage instructions needed to keep it from spoiling.

Again, you should also see any legal and safety information required by the locality where the product is being sold.

Concentrates

The *who*, *what*, *where*, and *when* will be essentially the same as for the previous products—who made it, what strain was used, how much THC and CBD it contains, the dosage, and any required warnings or legal disclaimers. In addition, the label should name the method of extraction, the purity level, and any expiration date.

One fascinating difference you will see between a wine label and its cannabis counterpart is in the way the package itself can communicate with the customer. Wine labels stand out with textured, embossed, and colourful labels. Brands can communicate their history, values, and unique attributes through QR codes, stickers, and innovative packaging elements. The truth is, *Vitis* has been set up for success where sexy showmanship is concerned. Cannabis on the other hand has not been dealt the same cards. While each market has its own regulations, it's common to have limitations on colours, logo sizes, and any non-essential packaging elements.

A WORD ABOUT ADVERTISING

Unlike all the other adult pleasures (alcohol, sports betting, grown-up—ahem—toy stores) in Canada, we don't see cannabis advertised on billboards, social media, or the giant blimps hovering over every stadium. That's because advertising for cannabis is age gated, which means it is allowed only where the people present are expected to be of legal age. So, you won't see advertisements much of anywhere but inside dispensaries or adults-only online and print environments, and certainly not anywhere near schools, parks, or other places frequented by children. I must admit, when my daughter and I are watching our favourite hockey team on TV, I wonder, why is it that society thinks we can be trusted to raise our children to make intelligent decisions about gambling and alcohol, but not weed?

In the United States, things are a little different. Some states will allow billboards, transit ads, and radio or TV spots for dispensaries or products, as long as they meet certain regulations.

A LABEL IS ONLY A BEGINNING

This helicopter-parenting style of regulation can be frustrating for those of us who want to explore new green horizons. When you can't see through the store windows, touch or sample the products, or research your usual media channels for information, it does make cannabis a bit harder to know. But that doesn't mean you can't find ways to learn or discover new products to pique your interest. In fact, this may be one of the things I love best about cannabis—it's all about the human connection! That's something you'll find at a dispensary, and that's the subject of the next chapter.

— 6 —

Let's Go to the Dispensary!

At this point, cannabis should seem less like a mysterious, shady lady and more like someone you could be friends with. You understand where she comes from, what makes her tick, and just why she has a bad reputation.

But if you're like I was when I got to this point in my perspective shift, you have no clue where to go from here. For most of your life, to get weed, you had to have a guy you went to, or know someone who did, and the purchase had to be made on the down low—maybe not in a back alley, but probably in the back room of someone's apartment. With cannabis legalization happening in more places every day, that is probably no longer the case where you live. So, what should you do if you're ready to go shopping?

This may be the best news in the whole book: *you can shop for weed the same way you do for wine.* Of course, don't forget to bring your photo ID, as there is still an age restriction.

SHOPPING FOR WEED IS LIKE SHOPPING FOR WINE

Let's see if the following scenario sounds familiar:

You're out running errands and your to-do list includes buying a bottle of wine, so you drop by your favourite beverage store. Take a moment to picture that store in your mind. Is it a big, well-lit liquor emporium with dozens of aisles? Is it a cozy specialty shop with comfy chairs in the corners and an eccentric clerk who greets you by name? A neighbourhood package store with a charming dive-y feel? Remember this image. We'll come back to it later.

You walk in and browse the shelves for a moment, looking at all the labels because you like doing this before you get down to any serious shopping. Sometimes, this is how you pick a bottle for the day. But not today. You want something new. You've entered the store with purpose. Maybe you have a get together with friends tonight. Or perhaps it is date night and you're going to cook a new recipe with your partner. Or maybe you need a gift for your boss's retirement party.

When you're ready, you will flag down one of the wine consultants and tell her what you need. She'll respond with a few questions. "What's the occasion? What will you be pairing with? What's your budget?" You have done this so many times you already have these questions answered in your mind. You know whether you need something to go with a specific protein or snack dip. You know whether you're in the mood for white or red. You know whether you like your boss enough to spend $50 on them, or if they only deserve the equivalent of a Two Buck Chuck.

You talk to the associate for a few minutes, she points out two to three bottles that she thinks will meet your needs, you pick one (or more), make your purchase, and head out the door.

No drama, no stress. Just a good conversation and a low-key buying experience.

You know what? Buying cannabis can be Just. Like. That.

SPEED DATING FOR STRAINS

Before I walk you through how to visit a dispensary and get shopping, I have some comparisons that will help you decide what to look for on your first (or next) buying excursion.

Once, when I was on a wine-buying trip in California, I went to an event they called a speed tasting. They had a table set up for me with glasses, spittoons (yes, I actually had to spit out good wine!), some crackers, and water. Thirty different wineries came by, one after the other, and poured samples of their products. With each one, I had just a moment to look at the packaging, talk to the producer, and listen to their sales pitch. Then they would move on, and the next representative would step up. They were so good I wanted to marry most of them, even though polygamy is not my jam. It was like a speed dating event.

Think of the information that follows as a speed dating, or speed tasting, profile of some popular products to get you going. I will use wine to give you a sense of the synergies between the two substances.

Incidentally, people often ask me what my favourite wine or cannabis strain is, and I swear, it is like asking which is my favourite member of New Kids on the Block. The answer is, um, "All of them!" (Although, let's be honest, Donny and Joey carried the band, right?!) I feel the same way about wine and weed. There are many variations that I love, and which one I pick while I'm shopping just depends on the mood I'm in and the experience I am looking to have. So, in the introductions I make below, keep in mind that these are not the only ones I like. It's just, in terms of prospective partners, these are a few that I find fun and approachable.

Also please keep in mind that recommendations are simply suggestions. The fact is, you typically create emotion around the strain you might try based on so much more than the flavour and the preparation. It also depends on your state of mind at the time of consumption, the atmosphere, your general mood, as well as how well the product was prepared, besides the fact that some strains will not be available in your area where other strains that I've never heard of are!

So with that, please take my recommendations with a puff of smoke, and let the speed dating begin!

Red Wine and *Indica*

I love red wine for its full-bodied awesomeness. Each varietal offers unique aromas, colours, flavours, and textures that give a sense of place and hints of history. Most reds have bold personalities, and their cannabis equivalents do, too.

Consider **Cabernet Sauvignon**. He's one of my best friends. Cab is an A-list celebrity with a great body and confident attitude, just oozing French charm. He has dark fruit properties like black currant, blackberry, or cherry, and sometimes a hint of tobacco, vanilla, and wood. He's a welcome guest when steak, roast beef, and burgers are on the menu. He improves with age, and the longer I know him, the more I love him.

Then there's **Pinot Noir**. She's an international woman of mystery who goes by many names: Pinot Nero, Blauburgunder, Blauer Spatburgunder, and Modri Pinot, to name a few of her aliases. While she might have been born in Burgundy, France, she's travelled all over the world on missions from New Zealand to Germany to California. She's a highly sought-after guest when the menu includes a pepperoni pizza, lamb chops, or pork. She is a romantic at heart and loves to wear a fragrance featuring vanilla and berries—though some describe her as smelling "like a farmyard." Her charisma and charm make that easy to overlook.

And **Shiraz**? That girl has my number. Some complain that her flavour is all on the front end, and she has no finish, but I think she has hidden depths. I love her spicy side, her unique attributes of pepper, berries, and cocoa. She makes a great ensemble cast member in blends, and she's a ton of fun at barbecues, hot curry suppers, and with cheddar cheese.

Now let's look at their cannabis cousins.

First is **Northern Lights**. She manages to be both fiery and sweet, which makes her super popular. Everyone around her is captivated by her relaxed, euphoric vibe. She combines an herbal, peppery, and citrus fragrance. Her purple and crystal colours set her apart from other buds. While she tells everyone she is from Seattle, there's a rumour that this *indica* was born in the Netherlands in the 1980s.

Blueberry is a keeper in my book. A child of the 1970s with an uplifting spirit. He can put anyone in a happy, relaxed mood, which makes him a perfect companion to wind down a stressful day. Known as Berry Blue to many, he gets his name from the delicious fruity flavour and aroma that he imparts.

And **Granddaddy Purple** only sounds like he's over the hill. He comes from California and sports a beautiful grape colour. Trouble sleeping? GDP will count the sheep for you, and provide a comforting warm, full-body buzz.

Both red wines and *indica* strains tend to have a strong flavour and strong, relaxing effects. They will relax you, but they may make you sleepy and a bit lethargic. For that reason, both tend to be more popular for evening use (ok, except red wine–based sangria), when you want to hang out on your own or enjoy a chill conversation with friends.

White Wine and *Sativa*

Just as white wines tend to be a little lighter than their red counterparts, *sativa* offers a brighter, more energetic experience. That makes both of them suited to social events, daytime consumption, or occasions where you don't want the fun to be interrupted by a sudden, overwhelming urge to nap.

Chardonnay is Miss Popular for all the right reasons. She's a world traveller who has a presence in just about every region where wine is grown. You'll often see her spending time around oak barrels. For an It Girl, she can have a surprising complexity, and the ability to be all business when the occasion calls for it. But her bubbly disposition also makes her one of the three most common base grapes for Champagne, and that's where she truly shines.

Want to meet the perfect wing woman when you want your dinner party to make a big impression? **Sauvignon blanc** is a BFF to shrimp salad, fish, and anything with a rich sauce (think asparagus with cream sauce). She brings a touch of class to the party by showcasing her famed Bordeaux roots. She's known for her citrus, stone fruit, and green apple fragrance. Her popularity peaks the first Friday in May when she is the guest of honour during International Sauvignon Blanc Day.

Then there's **Pinot Grigio**, a guy who is great one on one, but also the life of any pool party. When in France, he goes by Pinot Gris, which reflects his extraordinary ability to take on characteristics of the region he's in. He loves pâté, cheese, turkey, and of course potato salad. He peaks young, and unless you're lucky enough to find him in Alsace where he's happy to mature for another five to ten years, he is not one of those guys who gets better with age.

On the herbal side, **Maui Wowie** is the perfect beach babe. She has a way of making stress melt away. Her name comes from the sweet, tropical taste of pineapple infusing the bud, and her love of warm, sunny climates. She's a great partner for creative, crafty endeavours.

And if you thought **Pineapple Express** was just the name of a movie, surprise! She's as real as you or me, and she is a high-energy party girl! She's known for bright tropical and citrus notes, and for an upbeat buzz that starts quickly and has staying power.

Jack Herer is the outdoorsy type. He has a spicy, pine fragrance that drives me wild. His friends say that being around him gives them a sense of peace, bliss, and clarity.

Rosé and Hybrid Strains

The key to understanding this comparison is variety. Rosé wines are generally made by maceration, in which the skins are left on the crushed red wine grapes and soaked, which influences the colour and flavour of the juice. Rosés can also be made by blending red and white wines. This makes the rosé category remarkably diverse. In contrast, the classical French style is dry, for example, Italy and California are famous for sweet, fruity versions. This is why rosé is versatile and great for so many different occasions.

The same is true for hybrid strains of cannabis. Really, there's no end to the creativity of modern growers, or to their innovation in both flavour profiles and effects.

My favourite rosé hails from Provence. She's delicate and crisp. Her sense of humour can be acidic, but her honesty is always refreshing, and there is endless charm in her combination of floral and fruity notes.

And finally, let me tell you about **Gelato**—not the Italian ice cream, but the hybrid strain that shares its name! He's intense, but everyone he meets walks away relaxed, energized, and feeling no pain. Gelato is gorgeous, with vivid purple and orange buds, and tastes just as creamy and sweet as his namesake. He's a caregiver, too, and can often be found providing comfort and support to people with chronic pain and other medical issues.

Now that you've finished three rounds of speed dating, you have probably noticed that naming conventions in the cannabis industry can be . . . *creative*. I have concentrated on strains with fun, approachable names to match their effects. I have to say, however, that there are many strains out there with names I find a serious turn-off: White Widow, Super Cheese, and Bigfoot Glue, just to name a few. We have the legacy market to thank for this; many old-school growers had a wicked sense of humour, and they loved to celebrate their bad boy reputations in their naming conventions. Some contemporary growers have chosen to continue that tradition, but don't let a few crazy names intimidate you. In the next section, I will guide you through exploring the world of dispensaries, talking to staff members about your needs, and finding the right products for you. And if a pretty name is an important part of your choice, don't be afraid to own that! Remember, even in the wine world, there are some folks with a weird sense of humour. I have a distinct memory of trying a bottle called Cat's Pee on a Gooseberry Bush. The things we do for love, right?

THE DIRT ON DISPENSARIES

Be honest, when I say "dispensary," your brain conjures an image of a grungy place lined with Grateful Dead posters, staffed by guys in tie dye t-shirts, and a 6-foot bong in the middle of the store hung with a *Do not touch!* sign.

Don't get me wrong, those are still out there, and if that is your vibe, this Jackie won't judge. Legacy market shops are FAR from your only options these days. Some of them are just as fancy as a Tiffany's, with beautiful glass cases and sparkling lights. Some are laid out like pharmacies, and others feel like a natural foods store. Some have a hip, urban aesthetic like a nightclub.

This is the moment to come back to that image of your favourite place to buy wine. Close your eyes and conjure an image of it in your mind. How is it laid out? What's the colour scheme? The lighting? What about the space makes you feel good while shopping there? Now, just imagine transferring that style and the way it makes you feel over to the concept of a dispensary. My own personal favourite looks and behaves like a boutique wine shop. There are beautiful visuals of dried cannabis flowers on the wall, and the displays highlight features like regionality and aromas.

Like any other retail location, there is no real right or wrong way when it comes to décor. As a consumer, choose the aesthetic that makes you feel comfortable. If a high-end boutique is your happy place, look for a dispensary with that feel. If you feel safer in a space that resembles your doctor's office, seek that.

And if you walk into *any* dispensary and feel fearful, gross, or uncomfortable, you have the right to turn around and walk out. I want you to feel freer and more empowered in your cannabis journey, not less.

As far as cannabis goes, as of this book's publication, it is federally legal in Canada and governed by the Cannabis Act, but provinces have the final say over the products and how the stores can handle them. In the United States, cannabis remains illegal at the federal level, but the individual states have control over whether sales are permitted. They also determine licensing for dispensaries and packaging standards (such as childproofing).

These regulations can have an impact on the appearance of the dispensaries in your area. For example, you might notice that the windows are opaque or covered, to make sure that the interior can't be seen by anyone who isn't of legal age to enter. In some places, you might be allowed to view the products inside glass cases; in others, you might have access to only a display that lists the available products.

All dispensaries should have a few things in common, no matter how different the interior design or the music on the speaker system may be, or what the local laws are. I know, it's a bit of a bummer that you can't sample cannabis in stores the way you can with wine, but those are the rules. Packages should have excise stickers on them to show that they comply with all governmental regulations. Consider it a red flag if you walk into a store and see something that doesn't meet these criteria.

TALKING TO YOUR BUDTENDER

That's right, just like the employee who serves your glass of Pinot at the bar is your bartender, the employee who sells you your weed at the dispensary is your budtender. And like a good bartender, a quality budtender will take the time to get educated about the industry, the plant, and the specific products they sell. Cannabis industry entrepreneurs know that they are working in a space that is for many of their customers a strange new world. They should incorporate that fact in the hiring and training of staff. If staff members seem disengaged or can't answer your questions, this probably isn't the shop for you.

If you've walked into a dispensary with qualified, engaged staff, making a purchase can be easy and painless. You just need to focus on what I call the three simple, magical questions. You probably already use them when you shop for wine.

Listen, I can't tell you how often I get the questions "What wine should I buy?" or "What cannabis product should I get?" Really, it isn't that complicated. For years now, when I have been preparing to serve wine or another beverage in my social circle, I consider three basic things. Believe it or not, budget is not one of them. I put aside the issue of money at the outset, and I come back to it after I've found the answers to these questions:

1. **Why am I buying it?** What's my need state? In other words, what is the purpose of my purchase?
2. **Who will be consuming with me?** Will I be alone? Hanging out with people I know well? Or looking to impress someone?
3. **Where will I be enjoying it?** Will I be in my own home or someone else's? The park? A birthday party?

I've done this for so long that it is second nature; I don't even have to make a conscious effort. I instinctively start there. As a fellow wine lover, you probably do too, whether you know it or not.

If you are buying wine to celebrate an anniversary dinner, it's likely a very different bottle than the one you would purchase for a Tuesday pizza night. For a festive evening with friends, you might buy a 1.5 L versus a 750 mL, so you can share with others, or pick up a sweet rosé for a pitcher of froze. When cooking with wine, I bet you do just what I do—buy something you like to drink, so there's a glass for the yummy cream sauce and a glass for you as you chop and stir. And guess what? The process works just as well for cannabis.

Let's start with the need state. What do I want it to do for me? If it's wine, do I need a little cold refreshment on a hot day? Or a specific flavour to complement tonight's meal? My selection should provide a solution to my current need, whatever it may be. With cannabis, if I just need something to help me fall asleep, I look for a product that is quick and easy to consume. Since disrupted sleep is part of my perimenopause reality (and thanks a lot, Mother Nature), I keep gummies on my bedside table for that purpose. That's a specific need, and very different from what I might choose to consume when I want help to focus and engage in a creative project.

Question two: who? This is a big deal considering it is a small word. If I'm buying wine to consume at home on my own, it will be very different from the bottle I'm going to share with a business client. The cannabis product I buy will also differ, depending on whether I plan to hang out by myself or watch a movie with girlfriends.

The where? is a big deal, too. A night of Netflixing by the fire in my PJs is a different beast to a house party, which will require pants that do not have drawstrings. The context may influence whether I pick up a bottle of my favourite California Pinot Noir versus a more approachable blend, or a pre-roll versus a delicious, infused soda or gummy on the market. Innovation in that space grows every day! Trying them is as much fun as finding a new wine from an up-and-coming region or a new neighbourhood craft cider I can't get enough of.

(By the way, a business partner and I have launched a craft cannabis soda brand. If you live in Canada, you can look for Sheesh Sodas.)

Answering these questions will help you find your clear path forward. Once I've nailed down those three things, then I'll come back to the price. It's easier to set a budget once I know the mission parameters, and that helps me narrow my search even further. Instead of wandering aimlessly around the liquor store or dispensary—although that can be fun, too—I can go straight to the associate or budtender and have them direct me to the product.

TERPENES VERSUS TANNINS

There is one major distinction between wine and cannabis shopping, and it is grounded in the basic nature of the grape versus the bud. Tannins, the polyphenols found in grapevines, will affect the structure, aromas, and taste of wine. All wines have tannins; however, they stand out more in red wines. Therefore, they will always be a consideration in the bottles you choose. They will affect whether you like the basic taste, mouthfeel, and smell of a given wine, whether it will pair well with a given food, and certain physical effects it might have on your body. Thus, whether you know it or not, tannins will usually be part of the conversation when you're making a purchase.

That's not always the case with cannabis. If you are buying dried flower, then yes, the chemicals count. Terpenes, the aromatic chemicals in cannabis, will determine whether your product will be sweet and tropical or intensely skunky. That's definitely a key part of the conversation with your budtender. If you plan to smoke, vape, or cook with dried flower, then you should discuss with them the scent and flavour profiles that you prefer.

Popular Terpenes in Cannabis and Wine

Like zesty lemon and other citrus fruits like orange and grapefruit, **limonene** can affect stress relief and mood elevation. It can be helpful with anxiety and digestion. Some typical strains are Super Lemon Haze, Berry White, and Purple Punch.

Woody and herbal and sweet, **pinene** can have an effect on creativity and alertness and help with asthma and inflation symptoms. Typical strains are Harlequin, Blue Dream, and Jack Herer.

LIMONENE

More of a mango and citrus flavour, **myrcene** can relax you and boost your mood. It can help with pain relief, inflammation, and anxiety. A few strains to find with myrcene are Pineapple Express, OG Kush, and Northern Lights.

Caryophyllene is an intense cinnamon, black pepper, and hops flavour. It is a mood elevator and can help with muscle spasms, inflammation, and insomnia, and has antibacterial properties. Typical strains with this terpene are Skywalker OG, Sherbet, and Chemdawg.

PINENE

Linalool is your terpene if you prefer floral, lavender, and rosewood aromas. It has a calming sedative effect, and can help with anxiety,

MYRCENE

insomnia, and inflammation. Popular strains are Lavender, Dark Matter, and Tropicana Punch.

CARYOPHYLLENE

For other preparations of cannabis, that may not be a major consideration. The flavours of pre-made food and beverage products such as gummies and sodas are often made using distillate, which strips away all the natural terpene goodness. The good news is that more delicious edibles and beverages are being developed with their natural terpenes intact through the use of live resins and rosins rather than distillates. Marrying your favourite flavours with the natural terpenes of the strain used can result in an elevated epicurean experience. I would just talk to your budtender about the desired outcomes, effects you are looking for.

LINALOOL

READY, SET, GO!

Now that you have reached the end of this chapter, you have the information you need to go shopping for your first (or next) cannabis purchase. Seriously, you've got this. So now we can start preparing you for taking the next step toward autonomy, should you choose to take it: growing cannabis yourself.

— 7 —

Growing Your Own

I didn't start out as the nurturing type. If my high school practice parenting experiences are any indication, I would not be considered a successful nurturing type. See, in my social studies class, we were each given an egg and told it would be our baby for two days. We got to draw faces on the shells and name them. Mine was Peggy. Don't judge; almost everyone in small town Canada has a nickname. Anyway, for forty-eight hours, we were supposed to carry them everywhere, keep a log and assess the health of the egg babies, and bring them back in pristine condition. Well, let's just say there were more than a few replacement eggies over the course of two days. Although I may not have started as the nurturing type, my daughter's nickname for me "Queen of the Smother Mothers" would be accurate. (And, clearly, she gets her awesome nicknaming skills from me.)

While I might not have been a great egg mom, the experience would serve me well during my first experiment with growing cannabis on my own. I had been in the industry for six months and felt ready to take on a new adventure. I thought a little competition might liven things up, so I challenged my best friend to a grow-off. The rules were simple:

1) It was ok to get advice from others, but only we could physically care for the plant.

2)   We would use clones of the same varietal.

3)   Whoever grew the tallest plant would win.

The winner would pay for a spa day for both of us. We set a date for measuring the results, and off we went!

A FIRST TIME FOR EVERYTHING

If high school taught me that to be a parent, you have to break a few eggs, the growing competition taught me several lessons about DIY cannabis cultivation. First, in retrospect, I should have paid more attention when I was selecting the strain for my plant. When I got our seedlings, the provider described them as "a female plant with a unique aroma." Yeah. I was hoping for a berry or baked goods fragrance. Let's just say what I got was . . . *unappealing*. Like, *really* unappealing. I called my plant provider and asked for more information and was informed that the strain was called Super Cat Pee. I am not kidding. He explained that it was the only strain he had where he could find two plants of the same size. Needless to say, I named the plant Kitty.

When the competition kicked off, I was convinced I had a couple of great tricks up my sleeve. First, I would transplant my clone into a pot that I would keep in a wagon in my backyard. That way I could wheel her around to find the best light, shelter her from storms, or hide her from view if it was necessary. Genius, right?

Well, let's just say my relationship with Kitty did not end well, and it was definitely an "it's not you, it's me" situation. I was the absentee partner in the relationship, and I was unprepared for the commitment and her high maintenance needs. Kitty was strong and committed to her destiny, but my neglect stunted her growth potential. If I'm honest, I'm a solid two on a ten-point green thumb scale. Instead of spending time with her, I spent most of my summer at our cottage. To my amazement, Kitty flowered anyway. Now, next to my friend's plant, Kitty looked like a shrub next to an oak tree. (Now, I'm not convinced her husband, who has green thumbs on both hands, didn't help out at least a tiny bit.) However, I am a ~~good~~ so-so loser, and I didn't let Kitty's loss of the competition get me down. In fact, her perseverance inspired me!

The experience turned out to be far more meaningful than I had initially expected. It taught me that with a little planning, education, and commitment, I could build a beautiful relationship with cannabis. These plants are not like a cactus; it isn't something you can do on a whim, nor is it an endeavour you can take lightly. But growing your own cannabis at home can be really fulfilling and rewarding, if you take the time to understand her needs and growth cycles (like any good relationship with a woman).

For me, it was like something that started out as a summer fling, and then matured into my own seed-to-brownie adventure. It could be one you might want to try out too!

WHY GROW AT HOME?

If you are like me and value both control and quality in your life, then this is a great hobby to try. You have complete control over everything from selecting the perfect strain for your needs, growing conditions for the plant, and how organic you want the end product to be. It can save you money in the long run, as one plant can yield a significant amount of quality flower, and you're not paying all the packaging and mark-up costs associated with store-bought products. It also enables you to keep your use private if that's important to you. Feel free to borrow my wagon technique for quick concealment!

Growing is also good for the soul and gives a strong sense of accomplishment. It feels great to be part of the entire process from seed to harvest, and to enjoy the fruits of your efforts, whether that's your own tin of premium pre-rolls or high-tea cookies baked in your kitchen.

HOW TO GROW AT HOME

Here's an awesome fact: growing cannabis is an art and science. You will have your best shot at success if you follow the steps given next.

Plan

First, decide what strain you're going to grow. (I would not recommend Super Cat Pee, unless of course you're looking for an ultra-potent aroma profile that permeates your grow area.) As with dispensary shopping, there are a few factors to consider. Make sure the genetic strain you choose has your desired effects. For example, if you are looking for the effects of cannabidiol (CBD), you would look to grow a strain that is known for having high CBD yields, like Harlequin.

You will also need to consider the environment and climate you will be growing in. Like wine-grape varietals, different strains have preferences of humidity, temperature, and light to become their best selves. Some strains are better suited for indoor growing, while others like being outdoors.

A word of advice: cannabis cultivation laws vary by jurisdiction, and it is important to be aware of the laws in your area before growing cannabis at home. Do your research.

Prepare

Obtain the seeds you want from a reputable source. There are two types of cannabis seeds: regular and feminized. Regular seeds can produce both male and female plants, while feminized seeds will produce only female plants, which are the buds we typically end up smoking or consuming. Feminized seeds are a popular choice for growers because all of the plants will produce flowers. Feminized seeds are usually smaller and more round than regular seeds and have a higher germination rate versus regular seeds. They should be labelled if you purchase them from a store.

You may be thinking, "But Jackie, who am I to play God and mess with plant genetics? I only buy non-GMO food!" Well, that's up to you. But I can say, when my friend and I were in the midst of our growing competition, the plants took so long to flower that both of us began to think we had gotten male plants. I even felt bad that mine was stuck with the name Kitty! Turns out, they were just late bloomers and needed some time to find themselves.

Let's say you decide to grow from regular seed. You foster your plants' growth with love, sweat, and tears, but in the end, you get no buds for your efforts. Hey, you can still throw a gender reveal party, and there are still some uses for male plants. As with humans, they are essential for pollination and reproduction. If you're interested in creating your own seeds for future growing, a male cannabis plant is useful. Male plants can also be used for fibre production to make textiles. They have high levels of protein and nutrients and make great feedstock for livestock. They are also used for genetic research and breeding to create new strains.

When you have your seeds in hand, it is time to set up your growing area. Many people use a closet, and not just for the obvious pre-legalization reasons, but you can use any room where you can control the temperature, ventilation, and lighting. Most cannabis plants prefer temperatures between 21°C and 29°C, and humidity levels between 40 percent and 60 percent.

Plant

First, germinate your seeds. A popular way to do this is:

1. Put three to four layers of cheap, thin paper—paper towels are perfect—on a plate.
2. Pour water over the paper towels to soak them.
3. Place a few seeds down where they will lie flat and not move around. It's a good idea to put a little sign or label on each plate that indicates the strain name.
4. Cover the seeds with one paper sheet; you should be able to see through it and visually confirm the progress of the germination. Moisten the top sheet.
5. Cover the entire set-up with a second plate.

Keep the seeds warm by placing them near (not directly under) natural light or use a heat mat if you want. Check on your seeds daily and add water to the paper towel if it gets dry.

Seeds can pop up within a few days, but the timeline will vary based on the strain type and seed quality. When your seeds have sprouted long enough roots, you can gently remove the top paper towel and place them in your soil.

Nurture

Monitor your plants for growth and health, which includes checking for pests, colour, and pH level. As plants mature, they will need to be trained and pruned to achieve optimal growth levels. When flowers appear, keep an eye on them. In Chapter 2, I detailed the signs that show when it is time to harvest, dry, and cure your new buds so they can be used. The quality of the buds at harvest and drying time will affect preservation.

Now, respect your plant. Like a fine wine or spirit secured in a beautiful etched bottle, give your buds some love. Make sure they are properly dried before storing so they don't lose potency. Keep your harvest away from light, air, heat, and too much humidity—just as you would good wine. An airtight container like a glass jar with a snug lid is perfect. Alternatively, you can keep buds in vacuum-sealed bags in the freezer for long-term storage.

Growing your own cannabis plant at home can be a challenging but rewarding experience. With the right planning and commitment, you can produce high-quality buds that will be the envy of your friends. Hey, you thought

1. Grind

2. Fill paper

3. Roll evenly

4. Lick paper to close

they were impressed by your tomatoes and your roses, wait until they see this!

I couldn't resist including the illustrations in case you've gotten so enthusiastic at the mention of growing your own that you're ready to try rolling your own, too.

5. Push buds in at both end and twist the end closed

— 8 —

Socializing with Cannabis

LET'S SAY YOU HAVE A FRIEND WHO HAS NEVER TRIED A SIP OF ALCOHOL IN their life (I don't have any friends like that, but let's pretend). We'll call her Jane.

So, one day, Jane wakes up and says, "Hey, I'm ready to give alcohol a try!" She knows you're a bit of a connoisseur, so she gives you a call and asks, "Where should I start?" Well, you could just invite her over and start pouring her tumblers of your favourite scotch. But would that really be a good idea? Think about it. You, like me, have decades of committed training in consumption and enjoyment. Jane, however, has never consumed a drop. She has no tolerance. Her palate is not used to tannins, strong flavours, or that ethanol burn. Serve her the wrong thing and it could go sideways very quickly. You might make Jane seriously sick . . . and put her off alcohol forever.

STARTING LOW AND SLOW

If you care about your friends and want to give them the best experience possible, you aren't going to start with a barrel-aged whiskey, or shots of a third-rate tequila followed by lime chasers. First, you're going to recommend they start low and go slow in terms of ABV (remember, that's alcohol by volume). Maybe a bottled cooler or a fruit-based slushy cocktail. (Oh, admit it. You love them and I do too.) Or perhaps you'll open a nice, smooth Moscato or mix up a sangria and serve it with a good cheese plate. Basically, you'll give *Vitis* a chance to be her most charming, approachable self. You will treat Jane to a pleasant, low-key evening in her company; at the end, she'll feel happy and relaxed, and curious to expand her horizons with you again in the future.

This same approach works with cannabis products. When curating an epicurean experience where our favourite bad girl will be the guest of honour—whether you're hosting at home or going out—begin by considering the people you've invited to join you. Are they newbies to the bud? Are they advanced canna-sseurs? Or somewhere in between? Start with a low dose in a format with a friendly, approachable flavour, and consume it at a moderate pace. As everyone's familiarity and comfort levels grow (theirs and yours, too!), you can get more adventurous and playful.

A NOTE ON MIXING

Before we get into it, I need to pause for a little straight talk on combining multiple substances. Hey, I'm a lady who fears commitment. I often don't want to be tied down to just one thing. But once I do commit to something, I'm all in. And that includes substance use, especially while socializing. Sometimes I decide on pleasure by alcohol. Other times, I go for giggles via cannabis. Other nights I elect to go substance free. The one thing I don't do is mix them. Using both at the same time, or crossfading, can lead to a rough night. I mean it, think about the most overserved you've ever been—dizziness, nausea, the dreaded bed spins. Combining substances can crank up the dial on those problems. So, one at a time, please!

It's just as easy to add cannabis to your socializing as it is to grab a case of beer. And it can be just as much fun, as there are so many strains and preparations to experience. If you're not sure what product to choose, do what you would do with alcohol. Read about the latest varieties online. Search industry publications for reviews of new products, or updates from respected cannabis companies. Go to a dispensary and ask one of the experienced budtenders to help you pick something based on your answers to the three simple questions noted previously: Why am I buying it, who am I consuming it with, and where will I be enjoying it?

CANNABIS CATERING

If you need any further evidence that cannabis has come out of the culinary closet, you can just turn on your TV. Netflix is producing shows like *Chopped 420*. Cookbook publishers are starting to come out with books on the subject. Some of the best chefs, people like Joe Sasto from *Top Chef*, are doing high-level cuisine with cannabis elements in different courses. So if you aren't ready to "try this at home," consider seeking out a catered experience. These are getting easier to find in both Canada and the United States. Seriously, if you doubt me, go online right now and search for "cannabis catering" or "professional chef + cannabis dinners." If you live in a legal market, there's probably no shortage of these dinners being offered by innovative food entrepreneurs. These events have a lot in common with wine dinners hosted by sommeliers who speak about the provenance of the wine varietal, detail the attributes of each wine served, and explain what makes them a perfect addition to the dish served with it. Not only do you get to try some gourmet food, but the hosts also educate diners along the journey, detailing the terpene flavours in each strain used, and how they add to the taste, aroma, and effects of the dish.

Jordan Wagman has had people fly from across the globe to participate in cannabis dinners that he hosts. His multi-course meals use microdosing over the progression of four hours, with formats and terpene profiles carefully chosen to complement each dish. While he recognizes that not every individual is comfortable with the $400 per-person fee of his events, he stresses the importance of seeking out experience with food professionals who specialize in using cannabis as an ingredient, rather than cannabis professionals (or enthusiasts) who like to cook. "Do the due diligence and check out their professional profile," he says, "I see a lot of businesses set up by people who call themselves cannabis chefs, but really, they are nurses or firemen, or were in finance until three days ago. Just because you know cannabis doesn't make you a chef. Shitty food is still shitty food, even if it does contain THC. I appreciate everyone has different price points, but you also get what you pay for."

GOING OUT WITH GANJA

In addition to special, cannabis-oriented events, there's an upward trend in people who choose cannabis over alcohol for nights on the town. Some bigger cities in legal territories feature consumption lounges, where partygoers can find a selection of edibles, infusions, or inhaled products.

In my social and professional circle, I've noticed a huge trend toward gummies and beverages. They can be consumed quickly, taste good, and are inconspicuous. A friend of mine once told me about standing in line to enter a trendy bar in Toronto. As he discreetly chewed a gummy, he noticed others in line doing the same. I asked, "You were already going into a bar. Why the cannabis?" He responded, "The cost of beer and cocktails for the evening would have been $70 at a minimum. The gummy was $7 and low-cal. I spent the night sipping sparkling water and lime, hung out with my friends, had a nice buzz, and saved on the money and the calories."

For those who want to cut back on their social drinking—whether it is to save calories, money, or their dignity—tetrahydrocannabinol (THC) and other cannabinoids can offer an attractive alternative—as long as the two substances aren't mixed.

Get Home Safe

I know we're all adults here, but some wisdom bears repeating. Whether you're inviting people out or hosting them at home, and whether weed or wine is your pleasure of the evening, it's important to encourage everyone to plan for a safe ride home. These are intoxicants, and they have an impact on anyone's attention and reaction times. By designating a driver or using a ride service, everyone can indulge without concern.

Once you have a few chill experiences under your belt, you'll be ready to move on to the main event: hosting. Who doesn't love to have people over and show them a great time? Every foodie and oenophile I know will embrace any excuse to throw a party, especially if it means a chance to show off their culinary chops.

COOKING WITH CANNABIS

When I was in university and first experimenting with booze and weed, I was just looking to party. Now, I'm chasing a more sophisticated experience; I want to create truly memorable moments for my favourite people. It's all about ambiance and quality ingredients to stimulate all the senses. Whether I'm hosting small, intimate dinners or large holiday gatherings, I want to make sure that the music, lighting, décor, and, of course, the menu are all just right. That doesn't mean I can't still have fun—let's just say that the terms *potluck* and *high tea* have come to have new meaning for me! I have a great time planning events around cannabis, and that isn't limited to passing around a joint after the meal.

Chill Fact

Alice B. Toklas introduced edibles into the modern popular consciousness when she included a hash fudge recipe in her infamous 1954 cookbook.

It helps to think about in-home meal preparation as a spectrum. On one end are the people who can't even be bothered to boil water and think of their kitchen as a foreign country. On the other are those who subscribe to every available foodie magazine and watch *Top Chef* like it was World Cup soccer. You know, the people who turned their whole garage into a home brew operation. They have four different sourdough starters in their cabinet at any given time and have given each one a name. They have actually special ordered squid ink and used it!

We all fall somewhere on that spectrum, and most of us can easily pinpoint where we are. I consider myself an enthusiastic home chef. I love to cook, and I like to think I know a lot about food, but I don't run my home kitchen like it was a Parisian bistro. When adding cannabis to my pantry, I took that into consideration, and so can you. There's a spectrum of cannabis-inclusive food preparation, from super easy to advanced, and it is the equivalent of the difference between grabbing take out and making your own artisanal specialties from scratch. You do what works for you. On the easy end, this might mean buying a retail tincture with cannabidiol (CBD), THC, or a blend of cannabinoids. Some of these have extracts, essential oils, or other flavouring agents pre-added so you can just drop them into tea, coffee, or your favourite sauce. If you're always looking for your next culinary challenge, you can buy dried flower and experiment.

Any food you can prepare, you can infuse with cannabis. Anything from apples to zucchini fritters can be blended with flower or tincture. Culinary techniques have advanced, too, so we're not talking about your big brother's funky pot brownies made by mixing an unspecified amount of crumbled bud into store-bought batter from a box. Yes, you can still pulverize a flower using a mortar and then sprinkle it onto a dish—not something I recommend for beginners!

You can also decarb dried cannabis flower to make a compound butter. You can steep plants in a food-grade liquid base to make a tincture. THC and CBD hold up well in cooking oil, so you can infuse your favourite—many people like to use coconut oil. Butters, tinctures, and oils have a reasonable shelf life, so you can make them weeks in advance. They can go in any dish from cakes to pasta sauces to chicken parmesan. Thanks to better ingredients and elevated baking techniques, you can also have the old school fudge and brownies,[21] and they won't be something you have to choke down on your way to an unpredictable high. Now we can make the calories worth it by working with a decadent cannabutter that produces a truly pleasurable and indulgent treat and control the dosage to get a much better regulated effect. At the end of this chapter, I will provide some recipes to get you started. Some of these are my own; others are from industry professionals that I am fortunate to have in my professional network, such as cocktail and beverage consultant Trevor Burnett.

Jordan has excellent advice for canna-curious home cooks. First, he advises putting health and safety first. Just as you wouldn't cut up a raw chicken on a wooden cutting board, nor would you chop vegetables on a surface that had just held any raw meat, you should never add a cannabinoid product unless you know its potency to two decimal places. That means you should know it contains X.XX percent THC—1.09 percent, 15.21 percent, etc.

For your guests' safety and enjoyment, you should know the exact dosage they will receive from every serving of every dish on the table. He gave me an example: "Let's say I'm making a tomato sauce, and the yield is

250 millilitres/1 cup of sauce, and I'm going to serve a quarter of a cup each to four people. That means that if I'm adding 20 milligrams, and I emulsify it properly into the sauce, there's going to be a total of 5 milligrams with whatever that cannabinoid is that I've used in each portion."

Second, he encourages cooks to aim for what he calls repeatability. Tracking the strain, the potency, and the dosage for your dishes will allow you to make them to the same standard every time. Anyone who eats at your table will know the dish they eat tonight will taste as good as it did last time and will have a similar effect.

ENTERTAINING WITH CANNABIS

I have hosted wine-oriented events for much of my adult life. Sometimes I will create a food menu around a bottle I am dying to share with others. Other times, I'll pick a dish to serve as the centrepiece of the meal, and then find the best bottle to match it. I keep my wine fridges stocked for almost any occasion. I have a range of varietals and vintage years that span the world so I can pivot to meet the needs of my guests. What doesn't change is the importance of making a plan.

Here is the process I have developed for wine-oriented entertaining:

1. **Consider the guests.** Is everyone accustomed to drinking multiple glasses over a few hours? Or is one of them the type to sniff a cork and get a buzz?
2. **Decide on the serving format.** Sit down at the dining table? Mill around the yard and graze? Hang out in front of the TV?
3. **Create the menu** based on what works best for the format.
4. **Decide on the settings.** What type of serving vessels are appropriate to the food and beverage? Are we talking bone china and Riedel? Or paper plates and red Solo cups? I pre-set the glassware that is appropriate to each style of vino. I also pre-chill: 7–9°C for sparkling wines, 10°C for white, and 15–18°C for red.
5. **Prepare to add depth to the experience.** What fun facts can I share about the food or wine to add depth to my guests' experience? I always do a little research on the featured dish or bottle.

6. **Design the ambiance.** What décor and music will create the right mood? For me, that almost always involves Fleetwood Mac.
7. **Keep it safe.** How will people get home at the end of the evening? Make sure everyone has a designated driver or another safe ride.

When I began to experiment with hosting cannabis events, I found this process translates perfectly once I learned how to allow for the unique character of each substance. I have even started collecting the cannabis equivalents to my wine cellar. I have a variety of pre-rolls, gummies, and beverages to meet the moment. I don't keep it all in a beautiful hand-made box . . . yet. I'm actively searching for a sexier lockable storage solution than I am currently using!

With wine, the ABV is consistent, and my guests typically know how to set their own parameters for consumption. I just have to stop refilling the glass when someone tells me they are done, and to make sure there are plenty of non-alcoholic alternatives available. And if a bottle has a higher ABV than what they are used to seeing, I let everyone know as part of the fun facts I like to share.

When it comes to cannabis, you'll need to make a mental shift and focus on dosages. There will be some people who are brand new to cannabis consumption and may feel the effects from as little as 2.5 mg. Other people will want 30 mg. (You know who you are!) Some may have no idea what their tolerance or comfort level is. Your plan should include those differences in experience and comfort level. Again, it's about learning to divide users into three categories—beginner, intermediate, and connoisseur—and to classify each guest into one of those categories. Not sure where they belong? Just ask them.

Here's how to keep things low and slow for the Jane in your social circle. Let's use chicken parmesan as an example because it's one of my signature dishes. When I make it for a dinner party, I might decide not to put any cannabis in the chicken parm itself. Instead, I would infuse the tomato sauce that goes with it, and I serve that in a clearly marked tureen. This way my guests can add as much as they want. Although I've never tried it, I could dose the cheese that goes on top, and let them serve themselves. Either way, I choose a strain with the right terpenes to complement the flavour profile of the dish. I often choose a strain that has a sexy name with the desired effect I'm looking for as well. I have an affinity for the fruit-meets-pine aromas in Blue Dream and the citrus scent of limonene terpenes found in the Lemon Haze cannabis strain. I have found that these flavours, names, and effects align well with the food experience I want to deliver.

When the time comes to eat, I put a cute little sign next to the dish that identifies the strain and the amount of cannabis included. They can calculate, per tablespoon of sauce or cheese, how much they will personally be consuming.

You can do this with almost any food. You don't have to look for new recipes; it works with your grandma's meatloaf and the soup in your favourite chef's cookbook. Ina Garten has an amazing pot roast recipe that I just love to make for special occasions. Once the vegetables are cooked, you blend half of them into a sauce—yum! Well, it's easy to add cannabis to that process using butter, oil, or tinctures. If you are using a tincture, remember that alcohol-based tinctures are not always suitable for all recipes so I would stick with glycerine-based tinctures if possible. As a host, the important thing is to communicate what's in the dish, so that my guests are able to make the choices that are right for them.

Alternately, if I'm really wanting to let loose my inner Martha Stewart, I can choose an entirely different serving style and avoid putting any cannabis in the food itself. For those occasions, I could provide a little glass tincture bottle with a dropper; I like a THC/CBD-blended tincture, which I would likely purchase from my dispensary; however, I could make my own at home. My guests can pass it around and drizzle a little over different items on their plates.

The only limit is your imagination. For example, you could buy a set of pretty dropper bottles, dress them up with ribbon or paint pens, and fill each one with an infusion. As you set the table for the meal, put a bottle next to every place setting. Or pass them out as guests approach the buffet. Before everyone eats, explain the dosage that each drop contains. Your guests can add it to anything on the plate or in a glass. They are completely in control of their intake level, and they have a nice souvenir to take home at the end of the night.

Finding Your Groove

Substances and socializing seem like a natural combination. And there can be a wonderful symbiosis between them, each one enhancing another. But it can take time to find your rhythm.

It's not just teenagers fumbling their way into adult pleasures, either. When I first started out as a wine buyer for one of the world's largest alcoholic beverage retailers, I went to a swanky little-black-dress-type tasting at a trade show. I walked up to my third booth and introduced myself, discussed the wines with the vendor (feeling like an old pro), and picked up a glass to taste. I swished the wine around in my mouth, just like I was supposed to, then leaned over, and spit it into the spittoon—which turned out to be a silver business card holder. The spittoon was on the other side. It's funny *now*, but *then*? I walked into that event thinking *Vitis* and I were besties, and I left thinking she'd never want to be seen with me again. Finding my groove with wine took time and learning from experience. I found the same thing to be true with cannabis. I did a lot of slow, careful experimentation before I felt confident about how it fit into my life. But when I did, I became so passionate about it that I jumped into the industry!

It's also going to take you some time to find your groove and figure out how and if cannabis fits in your social life, and when and how you want to introduce her to your friends. Just keep it low and slow. Hey, cannabis is a pretty chill babe. I promise she won't mind.

Recipes to Get Your Feet Wet

Basic Cannabutter

The beauty of this recipe is that you can use absolutely any butter. Simply pick your favourite brand from the store. Or, if you're an ambitious home chef who likes to use the butter from different dairy-producing regions when different flavour profiles are important, do that. From there, the process is straightforward.

1. Take 1 oz of dried bud—whatever strain you like—and lightly grind it. Bake it in the oven at 215°F/102°C for 30–40 minutes. This process is called decarbing. The heat activates the cannabinoids in the flower. Remove from the oven and allow to cool.
2. Into a pot on your stove, place 1 lb of your favourite butter and 1 cup of filtered water. Heat and melt the butter, stirring often. As the butter melts, add the ground, decarbed bud into the mixture.
3. Over a very low heat, allow the mixture to simmer for

3–5 hours. Keep an eye on it and stir occasionally; the mixture should never heat above a slow simmer. Do not allow it to boil!

4. Remove from heat and allow to cool.

5. While still warm, pour through a strainer or cheese-cloth into a bowl. This will separate out the remaining flower particles.

6. Give the mixture a final stir, and then place in the refrigerator for several hours. As it cools, the water and butter fats will separate.

7. Using a spatula or slotted spoon, remove the butter from the water in the bowl and place in a storage container. You can pour the water down the drain in your sink.

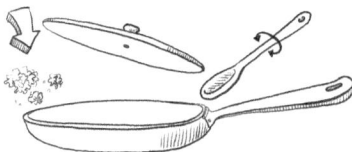

You will get approximately 28 one-gram servings of cannabis from this preparation. See below for the special modification I make in the cannabis butter I use for brownies and other baked goods.

Easy Infused Olive Oil

Honestly, it doesn't get easier than this two-ingredient preparation. As with the butter, you can go with any varietal or blend you like. You can choose a high-quality finishing oil or a lower-grade cooking brand. The ratio here is ½ cup of olive oil to 2.25 g of dried bud.

1. As with the butter, the first step is to decarb the bud in the oven.
2. Mix the flower and oil in a bowl. They will need to sit over very low heat (185°F/85°C) for a couple of hours. The easiest way to do this is with a double boiler or slow cooker. Keep an eye on it to make sure that it does not get hot enough to bubble.
3. Remove the infused oil from the heat source and allow to cool slightly.
4. While still warm, pour through a strainer or cheesecloth into a jar. This will separate out the remaining flower particles.
5. The infused oil will keep in the jar for several weeks.

Elevated Brownies

I love a good brownie! This recipe is my own variation of the classic mom's homemade type, so you can add your own tweaks or secret ingredients.

Ingredients:

½ cup melted cannabutter
⅓ cup unsweetened good-quality cocoa powder
1 cup white sugar
¼ cup all-purpose flour
¼ teaspoon salt
¼ teaspoon baking powder
1 teaspoon vanilla extract
2 eggs

1. Preheat oven to 350°F/175°C.
2. Mix dry ingredients—cocoa powder, flour, salt, and baking powder—then set aside.
3. Warm cannabutter over very low heat until melted.
4. Mix wet ingredients—cannabutter, sugar, and vanilla extract.
5. Combine wet and dry ingredients in a mixing bowl.
6. Add eggs and mix well.
7. Pour batter into a greased baking pan and bake for 25–30 minutes. Remove from the oven when a toothpick inserted into the centre of the brownies comes out clean.

Jackie's pro tip #1: I like to add 1 cup of milk chocolate chips (or the whole bag, I'm not judging) to the batter. You may prefer butterscotch chips, or nuts, or whatever. You do you.

Jackie's pro tip #2: Because these brownies are decadent, I almost always want to savour two of them, rather than discipline myself to stop at one. Remember, however, these are elevated with cannabis. To solve the dosing issue, I make a dessert-specific cannabis butter that uses 14 g in the mix, rather than the full 28 g.

VITIS COCKTAILS

These are courtesy of Trevor Burnett.

Wine Syrup

2 cups of red wine
1 cup of brown sugar
1 tbsp whole cloves
¼ cup whole star anise
Grated nutmeg (15 gratings)
Grated cinnamon (15 gratings)

Heat all ingredients in a saucepan on medium and stir occasionally until the brown sugar has completely dissolved into the liquid. Let the solution sit for an hour or until it is at room temperature. Strain out the solids and transfer liquid to a large glass vessel and store in the refrigerator until ready for use (label and date).

Bodega Sour or Sour Grapes

2 oz grappa or vodka
1 oz wine syrup
½ oz freshly squeezed lemon juice
½ oz freshly squeezed lime juice
½ oz freshly squeezed orange juice
5 dashes of bitters (preferably ginger)
*Optional: 1 egg white for texture and froth

Add all ingredients to a cocktail shaker packed with ice, shake vigorously, and strain into a cocktail glass straight up or over ice into a rocks glass. Garnish with a star anise, dehydrated lime, or lemon wheel.

Divine and Spirited Cocktail

1¾ oz whiskey (rye/bourbon)
½ oz wine syrup
¼ oz Fernet-Branca
6 dashes of bitters (preferably orange)
Twist from a fresh orange peel

Add all ingredients to a mixing glass and stir well for approximately thirty revolutions to dilute and chill the liquid. Strain into a coupe, cocktail, or martini glass and garnish by twisting another orange peel over the glass before you carefully rest it into the mixture.

CANNABIS COCKTAILS

Cannabis Mojito or a Buzzing Buck

⅓ mL THC beverage drops (Check the strength per drop for pre-packaged water-soluble drops and use according to your desired amount. Alternatively, you can use a tincture, although they don't always blend into your drink as well. Use an amount that aligns with your desired potency.)
2 oz ginger beer
1 oz club soda
¼ oz maple syrup
½ oz freshly squeezed lime juice
10 mint leaves clapped

Add ice and all of the ingredients to a tall glass/Collins/Hi-ball (remembering to clap the mint in your hands to release the oils) and stir gently to ensure the elements are evenly mixed. Garnish with a healthy bouquet of mint and serve.

Cannabis and Cider Sipper

Add water-soluble CBD drops (to your liking—typically 1 drop is
    equal to 1 mg)

3 oz pressed sweet apple cider

¼ oz organic apple cider vinegar (with the mother)

½ oz maple syrup

½ oz freshly squeezed lemon juice

1 oz ginger beer

2 oz club soda

Add ice and all of the ingredients to a rocks glass (short); stir gently to
ensure the elements are evenly mixed. Garnish with a slice of apple.

AN INTERESTING DINNER GUEST

1. Select your dinner style (sit down or grazing).
2. Create your menu.
3. Survey guests on drinking/dosage preferences (can be done via invite).
4. Consider the number of courses and the preferences from guests
    when infusing foods or pouring wine.
5. Decide on music, décor, and serving vessels (e.g., wine glasses,
    decanters, serving dishes).
6. Note things you can make or prepare ahead for time savings.
7. If you're making your own infusions:
    a. Make your infusions in advance since butters, oils, and tinctures
        can be stored for weeks safely.
    b. Label each infusion with type, strain name, and dosage.
8. Research and learn some great facts about your wines and weed that
    you can share: the history of the vineyard or grower, a great story
    about the winemaker or budtender, and any reputable awards they've
    won.
9. Set your table with appropriate glassware for each style of wine and
    any extras you may need for the cannabis, such as personalized drop-
    per bottles.

10. Ensure your sparkling wines are chilled to 7–9°C, white wines at 10°C, and red wines are served at 15–18°C.

11. Here's where the start low and go slow comes into play. Consider having the main part of the dish with a super low dose and having a sauce that can be added incrementally for those who wish to have more. Or you can simply dose the sauce, topping, and drizzle accompaniments and have each guest serve themselves.

12. Make sure that each dish is clearly labelled and discussed (dosage, what strain was used, why you chose it—was it the terpene flavours, or the effect?). I would suggest using a dosage calculator.

13. Enjoy!

Here's a simplified guide on calculating cannabis when cooking at home:

1. Determine your desired potency. This will help you estimate the amount and strength of cannabis to use.

2. Convert cannabis to milligrams (if not done so already on the package). You can do this by converting the THC percentage to a decimal. Then multiply the weight in grams by the THC decimal. For example, 5 g multiplied by 0.22 (22 percent) would give you 1.1 g or 1,100 mg (multiply total grams by 1,000 to get milligrams) of THC.

3. Calculate the serving size: Determine how many servings your recipe will make.

4. Divide the total milligrams of THC by the number of servings. This will provide an approximate amount of THC per serving. Alternatively, if you're like me and want to skip or double check your math, you can find edible calculators online like http://hempster.co/edible -dosage-calculator/.

— 9 —

Spliff Safety

I'VE JUST SPENT EIGHT CHAPTERS WORKING TO HELP YOU OVERCOME THE awkwardness you feel about cannabis and empowering you with my experience and information to help you decide whether or not cannabis has a place in your life. But there's a key principle that I need to share with you before I release you back into the wild. Fortunately, it is a simple one, a green golden rule, if you will:

> Pleasurable Consumption
> is Mindful Consumption

If you have as many years of drinking experience as I do, I am guessing you already know this about alcohol. And maybe, like me, you learned it after a few rough mornings. Now you know both the desirable and the undesirable characteristics of wine, and you know how to maximize your enjoyment while minimizing the chance of a negative experience. Better yet, if you explore cannabis, you now have the maturity to avoid a lot of those mistakes that happen when you combine early adulthood with controlled substance experiments.

THE PERILS OF CONTROLLED SUBSTANCES

I have said it before in this book and I'll say it again: *both wine and cannabis are controlled substances.* Both of them can play a central role in good times, relaxation, and fun with friends. But too much of a good thing can be very bad for you, and for everyone else too. If you haven't been living (and drinking) in a cave your whole life, you already know the undesirable effects that wine can have if you don't use good judgement. Of course, these include the well-known effects of hangover, impaired cognitive function and judgement, impaired physical ability, poisoning, birth defects and pregnancy complications, health risks, interactions with medications, as well as potential addiction.

Cannabis is no different to wine in that there is the potential for negative consequences of overconsumption to be aware of. Of course I am no doctor, so please consult with a physician if necessary and do your research.

- Impaired cognitive function and judgement: Poor decision making, accidents, and other dangerous situations can occur. This is especially true for children and teenagers whose brains are still developing.
- Impaired physical ability: There can be dizziness, visual impairment, loss of balance, and slurred speech.
- Mental health issues: Regular and excessive use can exacerbate or increase the risk of developing mental health issues such as anxiety, depression, and psychosis.
- Health risks: Consumption via inhalants can exacerbate or lead to respiratory issues including bronchitis and lung infections.
- Interaction with medications: Cannabis can interact with medications including blood thinners, antidepressants, antihistamines, pain medications, and anti-inflammatories, causing a number of reactions or negative side effects.
- Social problems: Excessive consumption can lead to interpersonal conflicts, emotional issues, job loss, financial difficulties, and legal issues.
- Legal issues: Cannabis is still illegal in many jurisdictions, and consuming in those places can result in legal penalties.
- Addiction: Regular and excessive use can lead to physical and emotional substance addiction.

These are serious things to contemplate, and you should absolutely bear in mind the consequences before picking up a wine glass or a pre-roll. That's what responsible adults do.

Right. Before you throw this book against the wall, run for the kitchen, and grab a paper bag to breathe into, let me remind you: You do *not* live in a cave. You already know about the downsides of alcohol. There are rules, and there are consequences for breaking those rules. If you have internalized the rules about alcohol, you can do the same thing with cannabis. That's what we adults do. We pursue pleasure mindfully in moderation.

RULES AND BOUNDARIES FOR CANNABIS

I'm going to spend the rest of this chapter laying out some rules and boundaries for cannabis consumption in more detail. I don't want to scare you off but to give you the guidance you need to make informed decisions. If at the end of this chapter you decide that the risks are just not worth it, that's ok. But I want to point out that these rules and boundaries are not any different to the ones you already accept with relation to wine. And I think it comes down to two really simple ideas: take care of yourself and take care of others.

TAKE CARE OF YOURSELF

I have touched on this in previous chapters. When you choose to consume cannabis, keep your well-being in mind. That includes:

- **Protect your body.** Avoid excess and watch your dosing. Choose the right product for the experience. Avoid combining with other substances. Avoid products that are not properly labelled, or where you can't tell what's in them.
- **Protect your mind and heart.** Consume in a safe space with people you trust.
- **Protect your character.** Avoid consuming in places where cannabis isn't legal or allowed. Avoid activities in which substance use can impair your judgement. You know, driving, work Christmas parties, cooking, heli-skiing, and karaoke.

If you think (or if people you care about are expressing concern) that you are becoming too dependent on any substance, consider getting medical and psychological help to fix your relationship with that substance. For me, as much as I LOVE wine, I could give it up tomorrow if my doctor told me to do it. If they made cannabis illegal again, I could walk away, no problem. But sugar? Man, they would have to pull those brownies out of my cold fingers.

Seriously, though. If you love anything so much you can't help but over-indulge every time you come into contact with it, it may be time to assess and get some help.

TAKE CARE OF OTHERS

When I say this, I don't mean taking away someone else's keys if they've had too many martinis. Although you definitely should. I mean you are responsible to make sure that your possession and consumption of controlled substances does not hurt someone else. For the most part, you can approach this the same way you would wine.

- **Avoid endangering others.** The most obvious is to avoid getting behind the wheel when you've been enjoying a controlled substance. Even if you have enjoyed only one gummy over the evening and you feel fine, it is better to get a ride service than to drive. And don't operate any forklifts, either.
- **Avoid compromising others.** Not everybody is comfortable with cannabis. You are absolutely allowed to have it in your own home, to discreetly consume it in public (where it is legal), or to share it with a group of consenting friends. But be polite; if you know your host doesn't approve, don't spark up in their home. If you are in a place where cannabis is still not allowed, and someone else is in a position to be held responsible for your possession, don't bring cannabis products with you into their home, business, or vehicle.
- **Avoid exposing the kids.** If you lock up your liquor cabinet, why wouldn't you do the same with your weed? Both substances can be very harmful to developing bodies and minds, and children can't always tell the difference between a product for grown-ups only and something

that's ok for them to consume. Did you know that in 2021, *Pediatrics* journal reported that more than 3,000 children younger than six years had accidentally eaten a cannabis gummy in the United States? They look and taste just like candy. If you have minors living in or visiting your home, it is better to secure cannabis products where the kids can't find them, or only buy what you will consume one dose at a time.

If you prioritize taking care of yourself and others, you are well on your way to establishing the appropriate boundaries for cannabis consumption in your life. Remember, I'm not here to scare you straight, but to give you the tools you need to choose for yourself whether cannabis has a place in your life and create that space for enjoyment and pleasure that fits you perfectly. If you follow that green golden rule—pleasurable consumption is mindful consumption—I think you will find your way.

Conclusion

THIS IS AN AWESOME TIME TO BE CANNA-CURIOUS. SERIOUSLY, THERE COULD not be a better cultural or historical moment for people who want to get over their weirdness about weed, chill, and discover what this beautiful plant has to offer. The science has never been better, and the excitement in the entrepreneurial space has exponentially increased the choices available to you as a consumer. It was a large part of the reason why I left a career in the proven alcoholic beverage industry for one in an industry that is still in its infancy.

It wasn't an easy decision. I've shared some of the life experiences that led me to feel nervous about cannabis. But paradigms can change, and statistics indicate that I am not alone. According to a national survey of drug use and health, 30 percent of Canadian adults use cannabis. Between 2015 and 2018, as legalization gained momentum, use among people older than sixty-five years increased 75 percent. Between 2020 and 2022, the number of female consumers increased by 55 percent.[22]

We're also getting more comfortable with open cannabis use as a norm in our society. Market research also shows that people have increasing concerns about alcohol consumption, whether it's the calorie count or other health effects, the environmental impact of production and packaging, how workers are treated, or the expense. In a growing number of cases, those concerns are causing buyers to shift their loyalty from wine to cannabis. A total of 34 percent of adults aged twenty-one to twenty-four years and 24 percent of those aged twenty-five to thirty-four years indicate that they have made the switch.[23]

I've seen this myself. I can't count the number of people in my circle who have been participating in a so-called dry January in the past couple of years—a trend involving month-long alcohol abstinence—and they are among 21 percent of participants who make cannabis and cannabidiol (CBD) part of their strategy for January. For others, the choice has more to do with their wallets; the $17 cocktail is here to stay, and even happy hour could end up costing you $50 or more. Two gummies, however, might only set you back a few bucks.[24]

For me, it began with a major shift in my relationship with *Vitis*. For a long time, I was perfectly content with mass market wines (and it's totally cool if that's still your favourite). But after so many years in the profession, I guess you could say my palate became a bit jaded. Now, if I am going to consume wine, I want it to be *really* good wine. If I am going to imbibe the calories and sugar, feel those *feels* the morning after, I want my favourite varietals and producers to be involved. I want the experience to justify the expense. If *Vitis* and I are going to get together, we're going to go big on quality and make the experience truly memorable.

I still chill with *Vitis* on some low-key occasions too, but cannabis has become an important go-to girl for my informal hang-outs. So, I was excited to find I could bring my passion for beverages into this space and use my industry knowledge to find solutions for consumers like me, whose needs and challenges had changed. When I started experimenting with cannabis products on a more regular basis, I began to see a gap when it came to transparency and authenticity in the space. Where was the beverage for women like me— the ones who valued high-quality ingredients, great taste, and total honesty about what they were drinking and how it was made?

In February 2023, my business partner and I launched Sheesh, a classic black cherry cola, in the Ontario, Canada, marketplace. We sourced cherry juice concentrate from a local farm. We selected a strain with strong cherry notes called Cherry Mac, which is extracted to make a solvent-free bubble hash, which is a product made from using ice rather than chemicals, to extract the cannabinoids from dried flower resin.

And we're just two of a growing number of entrepreneurs who are having a blast playing in this new sandbox and finding new ways to serve the customer we got to know so well as beverage or food, reps, chefs, health advocates, or working in other professions designed to help people live life to the fullest.

Education is the key to unlocking the potential of cannabis. When we're informed, we can intelligently choose whether it has a beneficial place in our life or not. I think this is truly the start of a new golden age for epicureans like you and me. Below, I'm listing the trends that I think will drive your options and mine over the next few years.

I'm eternally thankful that wine found her way out of the bootlegging, back-alley era of prohibition. Since that time, *Vitis* has found her way into the hearts, minds, and memories of those who got to know her and allowed her to step out into the light. She has certainly provided meaningful and positive value to my life both personally and professionally. As our stigmas and perceptions change, we envision a future of responsible cannabis use, providing hope and possibilities to nourish our bodies; meaningful connections; and a new engine for economic growth. Regardless of whether cannabis is something you wish to partake in or not, I think there's a good reason for all of us to raise a glass and toast a greener tomorrow. Below, I'm listing the trends that I think will help shape your consumption of *Vitis* and *cannabis* over the next few years.

TOP 5 TRENDS

Wine

1. The how will really matter. Ethical and sustainable choices in grape growing will become a more important purchase consideration. We'll see more natural wines from sustainable practices entering the market.

2. More alcohol-free, sugar-free, and low-sugar options will be available. Ok, these won't be for me, as I don't view them as the best expression of what a vintage can offer. But I can respect that others have different needs and priorities. Millennials and Gen-Z buyers have an

active interest in healthier alternatives. If nothing else, it will provide an alternative to just sniffing corks during Dry January and Sober October.

3. Direct to consumer (DTC) will grow, and it will be easier than ever to buy your favourite labels directly from the producer and have it delivered to your door.

4. Marketing will move to the next level in the digital age—I'm looking forward to holograms, VR, and greater use of QR codes to tell us the story behind each bottle.

5. Drinking less, better, and local. We'll drink a little less, but we'll drink better. Champagne Wednesdays, anyone? For me, sparkling wine—anything from cremant to cava, Prosecco to Lambrusco or my local Niagara Sparkling Ice Wine. Which brings me to drinking local: this will become more important as we seek to support our local wine producers and enjoy their unique local varietals.

Cannabis

1. Legalization will continue to grow in North America and abroad.

2. More and more innovative products will continue to enter legal markets. I've already come across hot sauces, gourmet truffles, cooking oils, and pre-rolls that use flower petals.

3. Education and awareness will continue to be a focus as consumers seek to safely explore their options.

4. Consumer priorities will shift from an obsession with potency to cannabinoid content. Currently, 60 percent of cannabis consumers consider tetrahydrocannabinol (THC) potency the leading factor when purchasing cannabis—but that's like choosing wine based on the highest alcohol by volume (ABV). Connoisseurs don't do it. Some of the most aromatic, terpene- and cannabinoid-rich dried cannabis flowers have low THC.

5. Edibles will continue to lead growth. Most people who are new to or getting reacquainted with the bud prefer a beverage, gummy, or other edible over inhalation vehicles.

In both cases, there are going to be so many new and exciting options to help keep our journey of discovery going. If you live in a place where both *Vitis* and *cannabis* are welcome, I hope you'll put down this book ready to go out and make friends with cannabis, as well as express a deeper appreciation for the one you've known so long. If you're among those who are eagerly waiting for the Green Party to arrive in your town, I hope you now feel empowered to walk boldly through that door whenever it opens for you.

Cheers, bottoms up, and happy toking!

Glossary

As an epicurean (see below), you probably enjoy exploring the specialized vocabulary surrounding the foods and beverages you love most. This glossary will refresh your knowledge of wine terms and introduce you to some of the key cannabis lingo. You don't have to know everything there is to know about our two cousins, of course, but a little understanding can go a long way to deepening enjoyment. And who knows, you may even get to a point where you can properly pronounce all the scientific names for the various cannabinoids. I'm still trying to master that; thank God for acronyms.

Annual—A plant with a one-year or single-growing-season lifespan from seed to death. Both cannabis and tomato vines are examples. And so are humans if you think about it.

Bubble hash—A concentrate made by collecting trichomes from cannabis plants chilled using ice and water. Unlike regular hashish, which comes in small bricks or balls, it is often sold in a crumbled form. Think fluffy brown sugar.

Cannabinoids—The natural occurring chemical compounds found in the cannabis plant. A total of 113 have been identified thus far, with the most famous being THC and CBD.

Cannabis—The common name for a genus of flowering plants, which includes both the species used to make industrial hemp and the ones that are used to make us happy.

CBC—Short for cannabichromene, a non-psychoactive cannabinoid that is being researched for potential therapeutic benefits.

CBD—Short for cannabidiol, a non-psychoactive cannabinoid. Often used for pain relief. It is currently the darling of scientists exploring cannabinoid health benefits, and of producers of small-batch, farmer's market bath products.

CBG—Short for cannabigerol, a non-psychoactive cannabinoid that is gaining popularity for use in edibles.

CBN—Short for cannabinol, which is derived from aged THC and may have sedative effects. Much easier to pronounce than most of the other cannabinoids in this glossary.

Cultivar—A specific strain of cannabis bred for specific traits.

Cultivation—Growing and caring for plants. Think parenting, but with less drama.

Doobies—A super 1970s cool name for a cannabis pre-roll. You know, a joint.

Drag—To inhale the smoke from a cannabis pre-roll or joint.

Dutchie—A Jamaican term for a type of cannabis pre-roll or joint that is rolled in tobacco leaves or other herbs, as opposed to rolling papers.

Endocannabinoids—Cannabinoids produced naturally by the human body to interact with the endocannabinoid system to regulate things like mood and pain. Think of it as channelling your inner cannabis.

Entourage effect—The theory that terpenes, cannabinoids, and other compounds in combination produce a more powerful effect than each in isolation. Really owns the mantra "Better Together."

Epicurean—A person devoted to the enjoyment of good food, wine, and other luxuries, like great cannabis!

Fermentation–The process of turning grape juice (sugar) into wine (alcohol) by adding yeast. You know, where the magic happens!

Hashish—A potent cannabis extract with a centuries-long history of production. Made by separating trichome crystals and typically pressed into a brick or ball shape for storage and distribution—before it inevitably makes its way into a batch of brownies.

Imbibing—To drink a liquid. The term we use to make consuming alcohol sound fancy.

Indica—One species of the cannabis plant. I like to think of it as the red wine of weed.

Inhalation—A method of cannabis consumption in which smoke or vapour is drawn through the mouth and down into the lungs.

Isolate—An extract that has been separated from other chemicals in a larger compound.

Joint—A cannabis cigarette, either sold as a pre-roll or hand rolled by the user. Often shared with friends.

Live resin—The sticky substance found on the trichomes of the cannabis flower. It is harvested using a solvent-based extraction.

Live rosin—A cannabis concentrate made by applying heat and pressure to the buds to release THC-rich output. Unlike live resin, it does not require solvents.

Perennial—Plants that live and grow for multiple growing seasons, sometimes for many years. Examples include wine grape vines and trees.

Prohibition—A nationwide, legal ban on alcohol in the United States between 1920 and 1933.

Phytochemicals—Natural compounds that contribute to the unique chemical composition of every plant. Those that distinguish cannabis plants include cannabinoids, flavours, and terpenes.

Psychedelic—A substance that causes an altered state of consciousness when ingested. Or the clothing and décor associated with people who enjoy those altered states.

Psychotropic—A substance that affects mood and behaviour when ingested. The THC in the cannabis plant is an example.

Sativa—One species of the cannabis plant. I think of it as the artist's best friend.

Strain—A subspecies of a cannabis plant, often intentionally bred for selected aromas, flavours, potency, or effects. Similar to the varietal when speaking of wine.

Sublingual dosing—A method of consumption that involves dropping a cannabis-infused liquid product under the tongue, where it is absorbed into the bloodstream.

Tannins—Naturally occurring chemical extracted from grape skins. It's the bit that causes your mouth to pucker.

Temperance movement—A social and political movement in the 19th and early 20th centuries that advocated abstinence from alcohol, especially in Britain, its territories, and the United States. Spoilsports.

Terpene—A chemical compound that contributes to aroma and flavour in multiple plant varieties and their products, including all cannabis and some wines.

Terroir—A sexy word to describe the soil, climate, and topography in which a particular wine grape is produced, and which contributes to the final aroma and flavour of the beverage.

THC—Short for tetrahydrocannabinol, the nearly-impossible-to-pronounce cannabinoid responsible for the high effect that humans experience when ingesting cannabis.

THCV—Short for tetrahydrocannabivarin. While similar in some ways to THC, it produces different biological effects when ingested. It is sometimes referred to as "diet weed" as it is said to suppress the appetite. Think of it as a munchie-free high.

Tincture—A liquid extract from the cannabis plant that can be added to beverages or food, or taken sublingually. It's like the hot sauce of the weed world.

Varietal—The type of grape used to make a wine. Comparable to a "strain" of cannabis. Each varietal contains its own unique properties.

Vintage—The year in which the grapes for a batch of wine were harvested, and likely when the initial beverage was made and stored. Think of it as the wine's birthday!

Vintner—A winemaker responsible for overseeing wine production.

Vitis vinifera—A common European grape plant cultivated as the primary source of old-world wines. It is used worldwide today. There are currently between 5,000 and 10,000 varieties of *Vitis vinifera*, though only a few are commonly used for the wines you will see on your store shelves.

Acknowledgments

First, I would like to raise a bubbly glass of prosecco to YOU and all of the fabulous and fierce people out there who embrace wine, people, and life beyond the labels. The ones who take the time to learn the beautiful stories, history, and provenance each bottle uncorks with an open mind. Your adventurous spirit and curious nature align with my own in a quest to embrace life's pleasures. Cheers to you . . . the courageous wine-loving rebel who took a moment to *Chill* and empower yourself to learn a little more about cannabis.

I want to express my gratitude to the industry trailblazers in both wine and cannabis. Your insights, stories, and expertise have paved the way for pleasure seekers, epicureans, and innovators like me to enjoy. Your persistence in pushing the boundaries to find greatness has enhanced our lives through unique experiences of the senses and added some extra giggles and laughter along the way.

A special thanks to Carolyn Roark for her collaboration, sense of humour, and for making me sound as awesome as she says she thinks I am. Your collective contributions have given us the opportunity to explore a world where wine and cannabis can co-exist as choices in our lives and just *Chill* and enjoy this book.

If it takes a village to raise a child, it takes a city to bring a book to life. I couldn't have done this without the input of so many. Special thanks to Joy Hallman of Stranger & Stranger for helping bring my vision to reality. To Thomas Beck for your illustration creativity. And I'm honoured that the book has benefitted from the contributions of industry leaders like Jordan Wagman and Trevor Burnett. The insights and feedback from all-round marketing all-star Rachel Colic have been nothing short of amazing. And I'm grateful to the entire publishing team at Ingenium Books—in particular publisher Boni Wagner-Stafford, who has been like a quasi-therapist through the process and I'd never have stayed sane otherwise.

I could not be more thankful for the amazing group of friends in my life. You're a constant source of inspiration, truth, and of course. . . .SO much laughter! I swear, if given the power, I'm convinced we could solve the world's issues with a Sheesh Soda or a glass of Napa Cab. In the meantime, we'll just continue to support, listen to, and laugh at (I mean . . . with) one another. Some of you are still working on not giving me the side-eye while holding your glass of wine as I sip a cannabis beverage. Please know that your unconditional friendship and embrace of our mutual success and crazy is appreciated.

To my family: I truly can't express my love and appreciation for your constant encouragement, advice, and unwavering support of my unconventional journey through life. I recognize that I must be a bit of a challenge sometimes with so many head tilting and "WTF?" moments. But know that I feel your unconditional love (and laughter) every single day.

Finally, I would like to express my deepest love and gratitude to my wonderful wife and daughter. Thank you for understanding that my relentless curiosity in wine, epicurean adventures, and innovation is more than just an occupation for me, it's a passion that runs through my head all the time and keeps me up some nights with excitement. The inspiration, love, and joy you both bring to my life were the driving force behind completion of this book and the work I do every day. I am forever grateful for you both.

Here's to laughter, adventures, and embracing life through a glass of wine, an infused gummy, or simply through the empowerment that knowledge brings us to remove the stigmas and labels applied to those who do enjoy them.

With heartfelt gratitude and a toast to life's extraordinary pleasures!

About the Author

Jackie is a product strategy leader and champion for start-ups and industry innovation in the beverage and controlled substance markets. She brings more than twenty years of industry-relevant experience to her businesses and clients.

Jackie is co-founder of Sheesh Sodas. Prior to co-founding Sheesh, Jackie was the category director at Hexo Corporation (one of Canada's largest licensed producers at the time and which is now owned by Tilray), where she oversaw edibles, dried flower, and pre-rolls. Her introduction of nearly 100 products into the market took her categories from fifth to first place market share in under a year.

Jackie spent more than eleven years as a buyer for one of the world's largest alcoholic beverage purchasers, the Liquor Control Board of Ontario (LCBO), where she launched many iconic brands into the Canadian retail space. In 2016, Jackie founded her own consulting company, BevPro Canada, Inc., successfully supporting new businesses launched into a congested alcoholic beverage retail landscape. She also served as VP of LCBO relations for the Ontario Craft Distillers Association, taught in the post-graduate Advanced Business Management Alcoholic Beverages program at Centennial College in Toronto, and spent a summer teaching in Denmark at Aarhus University. In 2015, she was awarded the coveted Drinks Ontario Industry Partnership Award, granted to individuals with outstanding contribution to the industry.

Jackie holds a bachelor's from Brock University in St. Catharines, and has completed executive development work at Wharton University of Pennsylvania Executive Education, Richard Ivey School of Business, and York University's Schulich School of Business, along with numerous beverage industry-specific courses.

Endnotes

1. Alison Napjus. "Pope Francis Doesn't Just Enjoy Wine; He Believes It's a Gift from God," *Wine Spectator*, February 2, 2024, https://www .winespectator.com/articles/pope-francis-calls-wine-a-gift-from-god.
2. Stephanie Pappas. "Start Date for Human Civilization Moved Back 20,000 Years or So," *The Christian Science Monitor*, July 30, 2012, https://www.csmonitor.com/Science/2012/0730/Start-date-for-human -civilization-moved-back-20-000-years-or-so.
3. Melissa Petruzzello, "Cannabaceae," *Britannica*, May 3, 2019, https:// www.britannica.com/plant/Cannabaceae.
4. Nikolay Andreyevich Gvozdetsky, Solomon Ilich Bruk, and Lewis Owen, "Caucasus," *Britannica*, April 9, 2024, https://www.britannica .com/place/Caucasus.
5. "Where Did Wine Come from? The True Origin of Wine," *Wine Folly*, https://winefolly.com/deep-dive/where-did-wine-come-from/.
6. Andrew Lawler, "Oldest Evidence of Marijuana Use Discovered in 2500-Year-Old Cemetery in Peaks of Western China: THC Levels in Braziers Show Mourners along the Ancient Silk Road Inhaled, *AAAS*, June 12, 2019, https://www.science.org/content/article/oldest-evidence -marijuana-use-discovered-2500-year-old-cemetery-peaks-western-china.

7. "'Cannabis Burned during Worship' by Ancient Israelites—Study," *BBC News*, May 29, 2020, https://www-bbc-com.cdn.ampproject.org/c/s /www.bbc.com/news/amp/world-middle-east-52847175.

8. Joe Dolce, *Brave New Weed* (Harper October 2016), 19.

9. Shoshi Parks, "What Does Proof Mean in Alcohol Content? And Where Does It Come from?" *The Alcohol Professor* (blog), March 29, 2023, https://www.alcoholprofessor.com/blog-posts/what-does-proof-mean-in -alcohol.

10. Erick Trickey, "Inside the Story of America's 19th-Century Opiate Addiction," *Smithsonian Magazine*, January 4, 2018, https://www .smithsonianmag.com/history/inside-story-americas-19th-century-opiate -addiction-180967673/.

11. History.com Editors, "Cocaine," *A&E Television Networks*, August 21, 2018, https://www.history.com/topics/crime/history-of-cocaine.

12. Mary Barna Bridgeman and Daniel T. Abazia, "Medicinal Cannabis: History, Pharmacology, and Implications for the Acute Care Setting," *P&T* 42, no. 3 (March 2017): 180–88.

13. Ryan Stoa, "A Brief Global History of the War on Cannabis," *The MIT Press Reader*, https://thereader.mitpress.mit.edu/a-brief-global-history-of -the-war-on-cannabis/.

14. "Discover the Lifecycle of a Wine Grapevine," *Wine Folly*, https:// winefolly.com/deep-dive/lifecycle-of-a-wine-grapevine/.

15. Nico Escondido, "The Man Who Discovered THC," *High Times*, May 31, 2011, https://hightimes.com/culture/people/the-man-who -discovered-thc/.

16. "Identification: Industrial Hemp or Marijuana?" https://www.ers.usda .gov/webdocs/publications/41740/15852_ages001eb_1_.pdf.

17. Jeffrey S. Graybill, Jayson K. Harper, Alyssa Collins, Gregory W. Roth, Heather E. Manzo, Lynn Kime, and PennStateExtension, "Industrial Hemp Production," December 21, 2023, https://extension.psu.edu /industrial-hemp-production.

18. Chloé Harper Gold, "The High Hopes For Henry Ford's Hemp Car," *High Times*, December 8, 2017, https://hightimes.com/culture/henry -fords-hemp-car/.

19. V. Butsic, E. Biber, H. Bodwitch, J. Carah, C. Dillis, T. Grantham, M. Polson, and P. Parker-Shames, *Cannabis Agriculture 101* (Berkeley, California: Cannabis Research Center, University of California, 2020).

20. Crystal Raypole, "A Simple Guide to the Endocannabinoid System," *Healthline*, May 17, 2019, https://www.healthline.com/health /endocannabinoid-system#cbd.

21. Elise Mcdonough, "The History of Weed Brownies," *High Times*, September 20, 2016, https://hightimes.com/edibles/everything-you-need -to-know-about-the-history-of-pot-brownies/.

22. Anne Bokma, "High Times: Here's Why Some Older Women Are Trading Wine for Weed," *The Hamilton Spectator*, February 4, 2023, https://www.thespec.com/life/opinion/2023/02/04/high-times-heres -why-some-older-women-are-trading-wine-for-weed.html.

23. A.J. Herrington, "Survey Finds 21% Of Dry January Participants Use Cannabis Instead Of Alcohol," *Forbes*, January 16, 2023, https://www.forbes.com/sites/ajherrington/2023/01/16/survey-finds-21-of -dry-january-participants-use-cannabis-instead-of-alcohol/?sh =320228aa42d2.

24. Ibid.

Other Titles from Ingenium Books

The Promise of Psychedelics

Science Based Hope for Better Mental Health

THE WALL STREET JOURNAL BEST SELLER

"TRULY VISIONARY, INSIGHTFUL, AND RELATABLE. A BRILLIANT MUST-READ!"
ROBERT ROGERS, PSILOCYBIN MUSHROOMS: THE MYSTERY, SCIENCE AND RESEARCH

THE **PROMISE** OF **PSYCHEDELICS**

DR. PETER SILVERSTONE

Science-Based Hope for Better Mental Health

ingeniumbooks.com/0ugf

Choices

How to Mend or End
a Broken Relationship

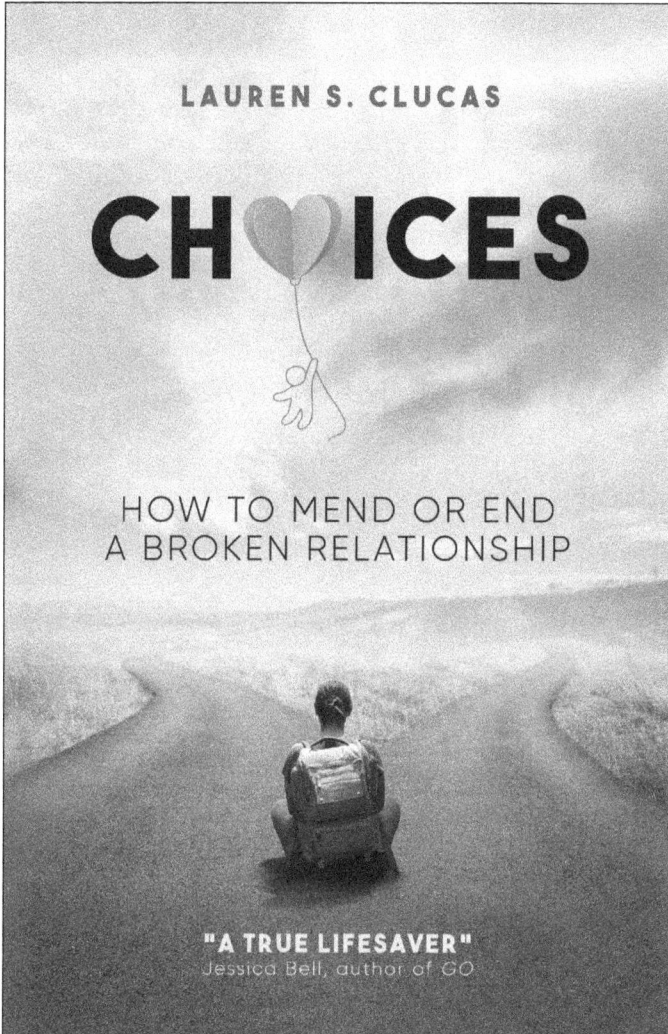

LAUREN S. CLUCAS

CH♥ICES

HOW TO MEND OR END
A BROKEN RELATIONSHIP

"A TRUE LIFESAVER"
Jessica Bell, author of GO

ingeniumbooks.com/CHCS

Choices Workbook

LAUREN S. CLUCAS

CH♥ICES
Workbook

HOW TO MEND OR END
A BROKEN RELATIONSHIP

"POIGNANT, POWERFUL, PRACTICAL!"
Verity Price, author *Present with Power*

ingeniumbooks.com/CHWKBK

Listen for Water

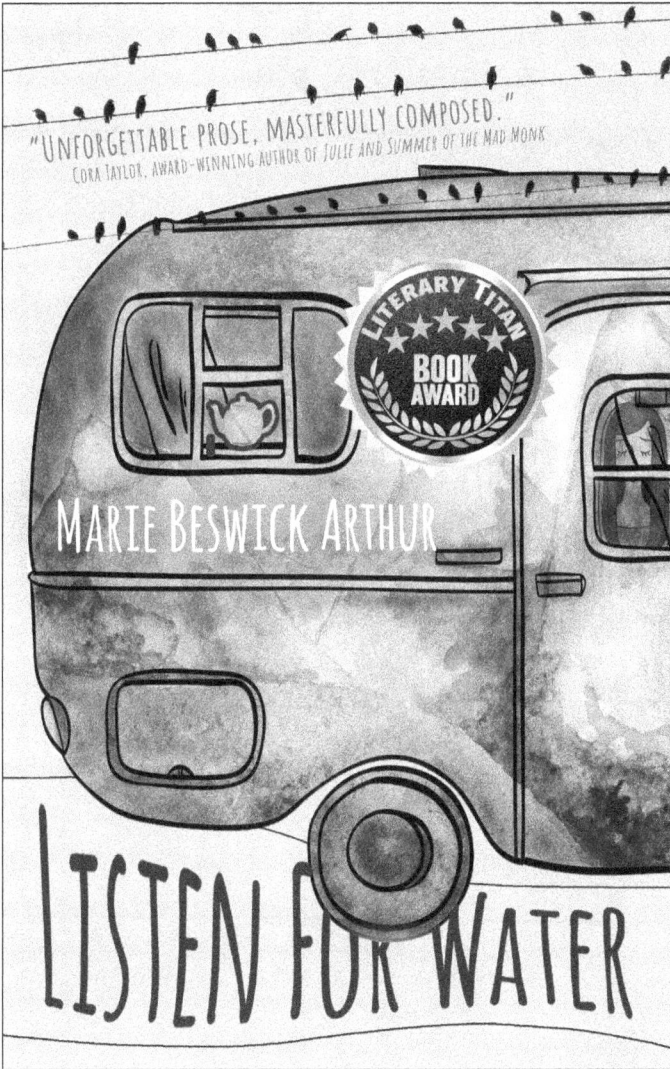

"UNFORGETTABLE PROSE, MASTERFULLY COMPOSED."
CORA TAYLOR, AWARD-WINNING AUTHOR OF JULIE AND SUMMER OF THE MAD MONK

LITERARY TITAN
BOOK AWARD

MARIE BESWICK ARTHUR

LISTEN FOR WATER

ingeniumbooks.com/lfwp

Four Fridays with Christina

Friendship, Death, and Lessons Learned by Letting Go

BOOK EXCELLENCE AWARDS
WINNER

Cynthia Barlow

four
fridays
with christina

FRIENDSHIP, DEATH, AND LESSONS
LEARNED BY *Letting Go*

"an unforgettable
journey of illumination"
Terri Cheney, author of
New York Times bestseller
Manic: A Memoir

ingeniumbooks.com/FFEB

12 Elephants and a Dragon

A Memoir of Survival and the
Kindness of Strangers

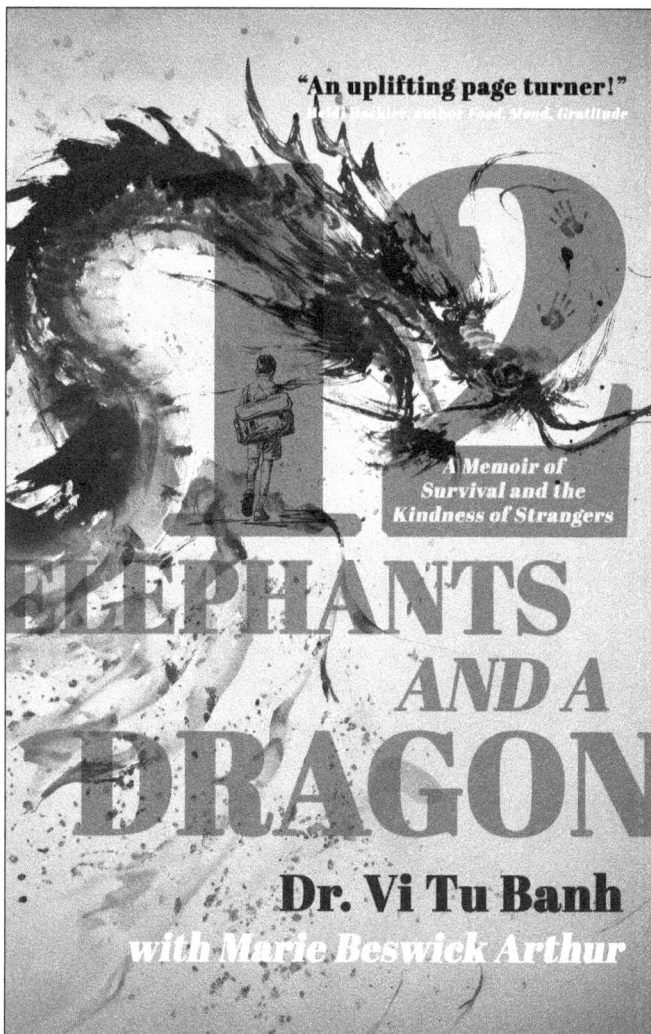

"An uplifting page turner!"

A Memoir of
Survival and the
Kindness of Strangers

ELEPHANTS
AND A
DRAGON

Dr. Vi Tu Banh
with Marie Beswick Arthur

ingeniumbooks.com/12ED

The Tortured Traveller

How I Survived the
Worst . . . Vacation . . . Ever

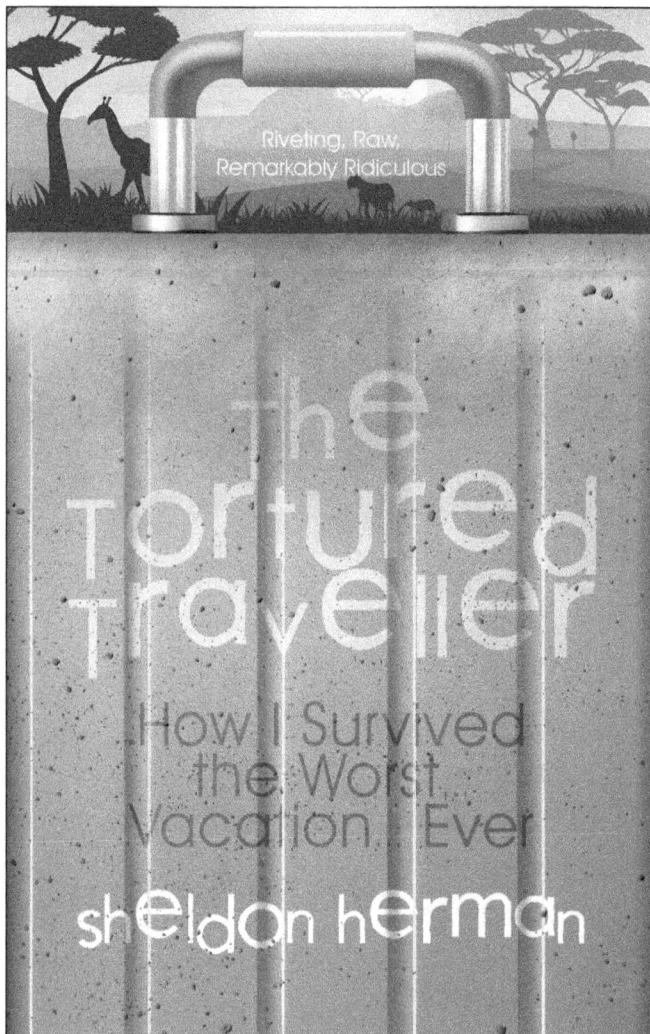

Riveting, Raw,
Remarkably Ridiculous

The Tortured Traveller

How I Survived
the Worst...
Vacation... Ever

sheldon herman

ingeniumbooks.com/TORT

www.ingramcontent.com/pod-product-compliance
Lightning Source LLC
Chambersburg PA
CBHW022100020426
42335CB00012B/767